Haggadah For The
Vegetarian Family

הגדה
למשפחה
הצמחונית

Fax: 781-639-0772
E-mail: micah@micahbooks.com
Website: www.micahbooks.com

Text Editors: Robert Kalechofsky and Roberta Kalechofsky

Production Editors: Robert Kalechofsky and Roberta Kalechofsky

Hebrew Vocalization: Debra Rittner, based on Hebrew text in Haggadah For The Liberated Lamb.

Printed in U.S.A., McNaughton & Gunn

Art Work: Dover Pictorial Archives Series: Eva Wilson, *Ancient Egyptian Designs for Artists and Craftspeople*; Carol Belanger Grafton, *Old-Fashioned Floral Borders On Layout Grids*; Stefen Bernath, *Floral Borders On Layout Grids*; Carol Belanger Grafton, *Children, A Pictorial Archive From Nineteenth-Century Sources*; Susan Gaber, *Treasury of Flower Designs*; Jim Harter, *Animals: A Pictorial Archive From Nineteenth Century Sources*.

ISBN: 0-916288-36-6

MICAH PUBLICATIONS

INTRODUCTION

During the Exodus, as now, food was an issue. Moses initiates The Festival of Freedom with the commandment to eat matzoh, the bread of the afflicted, of the disenfranchised, and of redemption, for seven days. Manna becomes the diet of their survival. Possibly the first recorded food riots in history take place during the forty years in the desert, and the issue is meat. "Let us go back to the fleshpots of Egypt," the slaves implore. Their cry rises to a crescendo in the incident of the quail, when their complaint for meat afflicts God so that quail rains down in abundance which the slaves eat with barbarity, and are then cursed with plague and death at the Camp of Kibbroth-Hataavah, or the "graves of lust." (Numbers 11:33).

Today, once again, diet is an imperative issue. Witness the public's reaction to genetically modified foods. The problem of a safe diet is now urgent for many reasons. Environmental issues are inextricably issues of diet as well as health, and neither can be divorced from a meat-based agriculture. The Union for Concerned Scientists ranks animal agriculture as the second greatest cause of environmental degradation, next to the automobile. Cattle raised for food take up one fourth of global land mass. The surrealistic number of chemicals, pesticides, hormones, and antibiotics used to convert them into food contributes to the pollution of our earth and our waterways. It is estimated that 20,000-30,000 chemicals a year are used to convert cattle into meat in the United States. Excrement from cattle becomes a moving river of sludge, containing thousands of chemicals and pesticides that are emptied into our waters and onto our soil.

A meat-based diet initiates a chain of events which threatens civilization. Overgrazing of land by cattle leads to a dangerous loss of topsoil and contributes to desertification in many parts of the world. Eventually spreading deserts and unsustainable farmlands cause famine, and farming populations are forced to migrate to cities. This in turn exerts pressure on urban problems of sanitation, housing, education, crowding, and health facilities. Half of all antibiotics manufactured in the United States are fed to animals, which contributes to the emergence of antibiotic-resistant diseases. Methane gas emissions from cattle contributes to 15%-20% of global warming. As Jeremy Rifkin remarked in *Beyond Beef, The Rise and Fall of Cattle Culture*, cattle have become "hoofed locusts." A meat-based diet affects every aspect of our lives, from the destruction of the rain forest and the destruction of topsoil to health and food safety.

The relationship between our personal health and the health of the environment is intimate and dynamic. In 1964, in her introduction to *Animal Machines*, by Ruth Harrison, the first book to expose the frightful conditions in the raising of food animals, Rachel Carson wrote:

> As a biologist whose special interests lie in the field of ecology, or the relation between living things and their environment, I find it inconceivable that healthy animals can be produced under the artificial and damaging conditions that prevail in these modern factorylike installations, where animals are grown and turned out like so many inanimate objects. The crowding of broiler chickens, the revolting unsanitary conditions in the piggeries, the lifelong confinement of laying hens in tiny cages are samples of the conditions Ruth Harrison describes. As she makes abundantly clear, the artificial environment is not a healthy one. Diseases sweep through these establishments,which indeed are kept going only by continuous administration of antibiotics. Disease organisms then become resistant to the antibiotics. Veal calves, purposely kept in a state of induced anemia so their white flesh will satisfy the supposed desires of the gourmet, sometimes drop dead when taken out of their imprisoning crates....The menace to human consumers from the drugs, hormones, and pesticides used to keep this whole fantastic operation going is a matter never properly explored.
> The final argument against the intensivism now practised in this branch of agriculture is a humanitarian one. I am glad to see Ruth Harrison raises the question of how far man has a moral right to go in his domination of other life.

It is irrelevant whether one eats the meat of pigs or buys kosher meat. The environmental impact from these conditions affects everyone. We all "live downstream" from the battery hen farms and the piggeries. Moreover, all meat raised for the commercial meat market, whether kosher or not, is raised the same way, on feed lots where the animals are fed similar food from rendering plants and administered similar chemicals. The tragedy of mad cow disease and the growing danger of pathogens in meat and poultry such as e:coli 0157, salmonella, campylobacter, listeria, and other food-borne diseases has exposed the rottenness of this system.

A meat-based diet is also the leading cause of many of the chronic diseases in Western countries: cancer of the colon, osteoporosis, arteriosclerotic diseases such as stroke, heart disease and hypertension. These diseases are major causes of our overwhelming medical bills. According to The Center for Science In The Public Interest, meat contributes to as many deaths a year as smoking does, about 400,000, and the secondary fallout from our neighbors' eating meat is just as injurious as the secondary

2

fallout from smoking---everyone suffers from the degradation of the environment, from global warming, and from the over-use of antibiotics. The cost of our chronic diseases, colon cancers, heart transplants and long hospitalizations for stroke victims affects everyone's pockets. Yet, to-date, there have been no responses from rabbis and Jewish organizations concerning meat as there has been concerning smoking, though they are the twin evils of modern health.

Diet is central to Jewish ethics, embedded from the beginning of our nationhood in the Exodus struggle. Diet is central to many of our contemporary crises as well, and therefore crucial to tikkun olam, the repair of the world. Eating meat violates four pillars of Jewish ethics; *tsa'ar ba'alei chaim* (remember the pain of living creaures); *bal tashchit* (prohibition against wanton destruction of goods and nature); *pikuach nefesh* (concern for human health); and *tzeddakah* (charity). A carbohydrate and plant-based diet makes healthier, wiser, and more economic meals available for everyone. It is particularly the inhabitants of poorly developed countries, the poor, the homeless, and the dispossessed who need to be schooled in vegetarianism. The relationship between famine, poverty, and slavery is historical and intimate. Most famines are caused by politics, policy, and neglect.

The undernourished, those for whom the problem is "bad food rather than no food," are an increasingly major problem in the United States. Dietary ignorance and mispractice has created a population of over twenty-five million malnourished adults and children. Only a significant change in eating habits can address this problem. It is easy to eat well, inexpensively. A family of six can eat a meal from beans or lentils, made into a loaf, burgers, patties, or chilis, with salad, rolls, and a rice or potato dish for about $1.50 compared with about $4.00-$8.00 (depending on the cut and portion of meat) for the same protein value in a meat-based diet. Vegetarianism provides a healthy, wise, nutritional, and *moral* budget for everyone.

We address this haggadah to those who will steer the moral and political course of the twenty-first century, for the issues of food and environmentalism will be on the agenda of their century.

Haggadah for The Vegetarian Family grew out of our first vegetarian haggadah, *Haggadah For The Liberated Lamb*, and can be read in conjunction with it by those who enjoy more extended passages. *Haggadah For The Liberated Lamb* is longer and has notes, while *Haggadah For the Vegetarian Family* is designed for an inter-generational seder. It can be read pleasurably by both children and adults. The Hebrew text follows the traditional passages of every traditional haggadah, but some interpolated passages may not be translated.

Permission to Eat Kitniyot (Legumes) on Pesach:
An Important Ruling

In November, 1997, Rabbi David Golinkin, representing the Rabbinical Assembly of Israel--Vaad Halacha--issued an important response to the question as to whether it is permissible to eat legumes and rice during Passover. One of the questions posed to Rabbi Golinkin was: "In the light of the ingathering of the exiles, would it be possible to eliminate the Ashkenazic custom of not eating legumes on Pesach?"

Rabbi Golinkin's response was an unequivocal "yes." The full text is in Hebrew, but the English version states that it is not only permitted to eat legumes and rice but it is perhaps even obligatory "to eliminate this custom," because it is a divisive custom between Sephardic and Ashkenazic Jews, because it diminishes the joy of the holiday, and because it has little authoritative sanction. Rabbi Golinkin wrote: "In our opinion it is permitted (and perhaps even obligatory) to eliminate this custom. It is in direct contradiction to an explicit decision in the Babylonian Talmud (Pesachim 114b) and is also in contradiction to the opinion of all the sages of the Mishna and Talumud except one...."

The custom of not eating legumes and rice began in the thirteenth century in France and Provence, but "the reason for the custom was unknown and as a result many sages invented at least eleven different explanations for the custom." Rabbi Golinkin pointed out that most rabbinic authorities opposed the custom. Rabbi Samuel of Falaise "referred to it as a 'mistaken custom,'" and Rabbi Yerucham called it a "foolish custom."

Rabbi Golinkin addressed the halachic question as to "whether it is permissible to do away with a mistaken or foolish custom." Again, his response was an unequivocal "yes." "Many rabbinic authorities have ruled that it is permitted (and perhaps even obligatory) to do away with this type of 'foolish custom'...."

Rabbi Golinkin also pointed out that by adhering to the custom of not eating legumes, it places an undue emphasis on this custom and tends to diminish the importance of the hametz. Indeed, in Torah, when the holiday is first pronounced by Moses, the food that is directly forbidden is leavened bread. The distinctions between leaven and unleaven were enormously symbolic for the Israelites, and we should keep this symbolism alive by remembering the original declaration of the holiday as "The Festival of Matzoh."

This decision has special significance for Jewish vegetarians who eat no animal products and whose sources of protein are limited during this holiday, but it is an important decision for all Jews because it increases the joys of the appetite and of eating from a table that represents the bounty of a bountiful Creator.

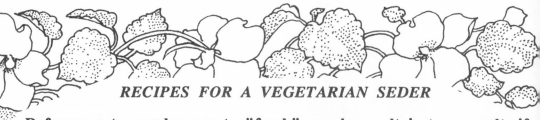

RECIPES FOR A VEGETARIAN SEDER

References to parsley are to "fresh" parsley; salt is to sea salt, if possible; pepper is to freshly ground black pepper; eggs should be range free from a health food store. If you are chopping onions and garlic cloves, chop together for convenience. Recipes are from *Jewish Vegetarian Cooking*, by Rose Friedman, which can be obtained from Harper-Collins or Micah Publications, and has 25 pages of Passover vegetarian recipes.

Seder Soup

1 large, ripe tomato	2 sticks of celery
2 carrots	2 TBS parsley
1 small onion	Salt & pepper
2 leeks	1 vegetable stock cube (optional)
1 small potato	10-12 1/2 cups of water
1 small parsnip	

1. Wash vegetables, cut into small pieces.
2. Simmer vegetables in water for about 1-1 1/2 hours.
3. Add parsley, seasonings & vegetable cube.
4. Add your favorite matzoh farfel.

Seder Roast

1 1/2 cups mixed ground nuts	1/2 cup of matzoh meal
2 eggs, beaten	2 TBS tomato paste
1 medium onion, chopped	salt & pepper to taste
1-2 cloves of garlic, chopped	1 large onion, sliced
1 large carrot, grated	2 1/2 cups of vegetable stock

1. Mix all ingredients, except sliced onion and vegetable stock.
2. Grease an ovenproof casserole well, place a layer of sliced onions on bottom and sides, place nut mixture on top of onions.
3. Pour half the vegetable stock over nut mixture.
4. Bake at 350 for about 45 minutes.
5. Baste mixture with the rest of the stock about every fifteen minutes. The secret of success of this recipe is to keep it moist.
6. If this recipe is doubled, use only 3 eggs, or the equivalent.

Oven-fried potatoes or your favorite potato kugel go well with seder roast.

Merren Tzimmes

2 medium onions, grated or chopped
2 cloves of garlic, crushed
2 TBS vegetable oil
1 pound of carrots, grated
3 TBS ground almonds

1 tsp lemon juice
1 egg, beaten
salt & pepper to taste
1/4 tsp ground nutmeg
1/2 cup matzoh meal

1. Sauté grated onion and garlic until golden & transparent.
2. Add grated carrots, cook for another 5 minutes, stirring continuously. Remove from heat.
3. Combine with ground almonds, lemon juice, egg & seasonings, mixing well.
4. Add enough matzoh meal to make a firm consistency.
5. Put in greased overproof casserole; bake at 375 for about 30 minutes.

Burriklach Mit Merralach(beets and carrots)

3 medium beets, uncooked
3 carrots
2 eating apples
2 TBS parsley

2 TBS olive oil
1 TBS. lemon juice
salt & pepper

1. Peel & grate beets, carrots & apples.
2. Mix olive oil, lemon juice & seasonings together, pour over the salad. Add more oil & lemon juice if desired.
3. Sprinkle with parsley.

Chametz: Searching for leavened products. Take a few days to do this, and combine it with spring cleaning chores. As you rid the house of chametz also rid the house of products containing meat and "products of pain": cosmetics and household products that have animal ingredients in them or have been tested on animals. Make your house a "bayit shalom," a house of peace for the holiday. Involve your children in the process and use the occasion to teach them the tradition of tsa'ar ba'alei chayim, how to read labels, and how to become responsible consumers. It is also a good time to teach them about slavery, and that it exists in the modern world. Material about slavery can be ordered from the Anti-Slavery Society, 180 Brixton Road, London SW9 6AT, England. To have material available, order well in advance. It is important to know that enslavement of children, women, chattel, bondage, and debt slavery still exist in many parts of the world, and go unnoticed by Western societies. Wherever unyielding poverty and famine exist, slavery exists. It is the travelling companion of desperation. Use the occasion to protest _all_ trafficking in living flesh of _all_ creatures. The association between animal rights and abolition of _all_ slavery is historic. In the nineteenth century many of the great social reformers who fought for abolition, women's right, prison reform and the elimination of child abuse also fought for animal rights. As a modern day abolitionist stated it in a splendid phrase, "This was the genealogy of social reform."

Table Setting: The table should be set with beauty, with flowers, greenery, candles, and the Cup for Elijah

The seder plate: bitter herbs (which can be horse radish), charoshes (a mixture of chopped nuts, apples, wine and cinammon), greens for dipping (can be parsley). In place of the shankbone, a beet can be used. (Talmud, Tractate Pesahim 114b). We recommend several olives placed next to several grapes and matzoh crumbs that have been wrapped in saran wrap so that no moisture can reach them. The purpose of these three foods is their relationship to the passage in Deuteronomy (24: 19-25: 4) which instructs us to leave the second shaking of the vine tree for the poor and the second shaking of the olive tree for the poor. In the following passage we are also instructed "Not to muzzle the ox when it treads out the grain in the fields." We call these the "Mitzvoth of Compassion for oppressed creatures," and offer them in place of the shankbone, in the spirit in which Rabbi Ben

Zakkai instructed his disciples to practise "prayer and deeds of loving kindness in place of sacrifice." In this spirit of *remembering*, some vegetarian families place a drawing or papier maché lamb. It is a lovely ceremony to place this replica in the midst of the olives, grapes and unfermented grain and say: "We remember the lamb that was sacrificed but in the spirit of Rav Ben Zakkai and instructed by our prophets on the superiority of justice, mercy and righteousness over deeds of blood sacrifice, we will do deeds of mercy, justice and loving kindness in place of sacrifice and call this holiday by its original name, Hag ha Matzoh, the Festival of Freedom.

The Roasted Egg: There is no halachic requirement for a roasted egg, It is a custom which symbolized the *hagigah* or festival offering as well as spring and life. However, it would be a travesty to use an egg from a chicken which has spent its short life in death-like circumstances to symbolize freedom, spring, hope and life. Hag ha matzoh has developed many customs over the centuries, and you may wish to replace the roasted egg with another custom: a crocus or an egg made of papier maché, or drawing of an egg which children can decorate with flowers.

The four cups of wine are drunk in the following order: The Sanctification of the Day; the Sanctification of Creation; the Sanctification of Israel; the Cup of Redemption. A fifth cup of wine can be drunk after the meal.

Three portions of matzoh under a cover. The middle portion is the aphikomen, to share later and to scatter outdoors.

Bowls of salt water for the dipping of the greens.

Large bowl of water with paper towels for washing and drying hands. It is nice to put flower petals in the water.

An empty chair is customary. It symbolizes welcome for others who cannot attend.

ORDER OF THE MEAL

Lighting of the Candles

U'rhatz: Washing of Hands. Pass bowls of water and towels.

Kos Kiddush: Sanctification of Day: First Cup of Wine

Yahatz: The Bread of Affliction and setting aside the aphikomen

Maror: Eating of bitter herbs

Charoshes: Mixture of chopped apples and nuts moistened with wine and flavored with cinammon. Charoshes refers to the mortar with which the Hebrews made their bricks. It is a good example of how symbols sometimes become transformed and even reverse their meaning. Charoshes also symbolizes the sweetness of life, and some people eat it with maror to symbolize the bitter and the sweet in life.

The Four Questions

Karpas: Dipping of greens

Sanctification of Creation: Second cup of wine

Maggid: recital of text

Sanctification of Israel: Third Cup of Wine
The Cup of Redemption: The Fourth Cup of Wine

Meal Is Served

Grace and Thanksgiving: Participants gather at the open door, share the aphikomen and toss outside, symbolizing charity in feeding all God's creatures. Cup of Elijah is raised to the outdoor for tikkun olam, our hope for the future. The final psalms are great hymns to nature, a feast of language for the soul searching to express the grandeur of God's creation.

9

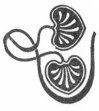

KADDESH: Sanctification of the Day

You shall keep the feast of Hag ha Matzoh, for on this day I brought you out of the house of bondage. You shall observe this day throughout the generations and tell the story of this miraculous redemption to your children, and instruct them to tell it to their children, so that you may remember your Creator and My glorious works forever.

Blessed art Thou Sovereign of the World, Eternal
Creator of the Universe and Sustainer of all that lives
Blessed art Thou Who has given great gifts to Your people:
Torah, covenant, mitzvoth, redemption and righteousness,
Whose mercy is for all Your creatures and all that lives.
Blessed art Thou Who teaches us that all life is sacred;
Blessed art Thou Who has preserved us to this day,
Who bids us celebrate Hag Ha Matzoh,
Festival of Freedom and Redemption

With a mighty hand You brought us out of bondage,
Out of the desert and across the seas.
We pray to be worthy of Your gifts
That we not become a painful memory to You.
For why did You redeem us
If not to glorify Your name
And the earth Your creation
And all Your creatures in it.

Turn, turn, and turn again
We return to You as the seasons return.

In loving kindness You have redeemed us again and again,
In loving kindness You brought Your creatures before Adam,
and not one was afraid;
In loving kindness You instructed Noah to build an ark
and save each kind from among Your creatures.

Neither are we so hard hearted as to believe
that the earth was created for us alone.
Your compassion is enduring for all life.

We place olives, grapes, and unfermented barley here, symbols of Your mitzvoth to us to help the oppressed and the enslaved. We remember the lamb that was sacrificed on the eve of our

קַדֵּשׁ: לְקָדוֹשׁ הַיּוֹם

וּשְׁמַרְתֶּם אֶת יוֹם חַג הַמַּצּוֹת כִּי בַּיּוֹם הַזֶּה הוֹצֵאתִיכֶם מִבֵּית עֲבָדִים.
וּשְׁמַרְתֶּם אֶת הַיּוֹם הַזֶּה וְאֶת הַחַג הַזֶּה לְדוֹרוֹתֵיכֶם
וְהִגַּדְתֶּם אֶת סִפּוּר הַגְּאֻלָּה לְיַלְדֵיכֶם. וְהֵם יְסַפְּרוּהוּ לְיַלְדֵיהֶם לְמַעַן
תִּזְכְּרוּ אֶת תִּפְאֶרֶת מַעֲשַׂי.

בָּרוּךְ אַתָּה יְיָ אֱלֹהֵינוּ מֶלֶךְ הָעוֹלָם. בּוֹרְאוֹ הַנִּצְחִי שֶׁל הַיְקוּם
הַזָּן אֶת כָּל חַי
בָּרוּךְ אַתָּה שֶׁהֶעֱנַקְתָּ לְעַמְּךָ יִשְׂרָאֵל מֵחַסְדֶּיךָ.
תּוֹרָה, בְּרִית, מִצְווֹת, גְּאֻלָּה וָצֶדֶק.
שֶׁרַחֲמֶיךָ עַל כָּל יְצוּרֶיךָ וְעַל כָּל חַי
בָּרוּךְ אַתָּה הַמְלַמְּדֵנוּ אֶת קְדֻשַּׁת כָּל חַי:
בָּרוּךְ אַתָּה שֶׁקִּיְּמָנוּ לַיּוֹם הַזֶּה
אַתָּה, שֶׁצִּוִּיתָנוּ לָחוֹג אֶת חַג הַמַּצּוֹת
חַג הַחֵרוּת וְהַגְּאֻלָּה

בְּיָד חֲזָקָה הוֹצֵאתָנוּ מִבֵּית עֲבָדִים.
דֶּרֶךְ מִדְבָּר וְיַמִּים.
וְאָנוּ תְּפִילָה שֶׁנִּזְכֶּה לַחַסְדֶּיךָ.
שֶׁלֹּא נִהְיֶה לְזִכָּרוֹן מַכְאִיב.
שֶׁהֲרֵי גְּאַלְתָּנוּ
לְמַעַן נְפָאֵר אֶת שְׁמֶךָ
וְאֶת הָאָרֶץ שֶׁבָּרָאתָ
וְאֶת כָּל יְצוּרֶיךָ שֶׁעָלֶיהָ.

סֹב, סֹב,   שׁוּב בָּסֹב
אֵלֶיךָ נָסֹב כְּדַרְךְ שֶׁנִּסֹּבּוֹת עוֹנוֹת הַשָּׁנָה
בְּאַהֲבָה וּבְרָצוֹן גְּאַלְתָּנוּ פַּעַם אַחַר פַּעַם.
בְּאַהֲבָה וּבְרָצוֹן הֵבֵאתָ אֶת יְצוּרֶיךָ לִפְנֵי אָדָם.
וְאַף לֹא אֶחָד מֵהֶם נֶחֱרַד,
בְּאַהֲבָה וּבְרָצוֹן צִוִּיתָ אֶת נֹחַ לִבְנוֹת אֶת הַתֵּבָה
וּלְהַצִּיל אֶת כָּל הַחַי לְמִינֵהוּ
וְלֹא נִקְשָׁה אֶת לִבֵּנוּ
לְהַאֲמִין כִּי הָאָרֶץ שֶׁבָּרָאתָ
לָנוּ הִיא בִּלְבַד.

redemption from slavery, but as free people, we say with the prophets:

I desire kindness and not sacrifice
I desire the love of God and not burnt offerings

LIGHTING OF THE CANDLES

Baruch Atah Adonoi Eloheinu Melech Ha-olam asher kidshanu b'mitzvo-tav v'tzivanu l'hadlik neir shel (shabbat v'shel) yom tov.

In praising God we say that all life is sacred. Let us live in this wisdom: to heal and not to harm, to revere and to sanctify and not abuse, to choose life for all You gave life to.

(For Friday evenings: Remember the Sabbath and keep it holy. Six days you may work, but the seventh day is consecrated to Me, Your God. You shall cease from all labor on this day, so that your ox and your ass may rest (Exod. 23:12). You shall not do any work on this day, neither your son, nor your daughter, nor your manservant, nor your cattle, nor the stranger that is within your gates: for in six days I made heaven and earth, the sea, and all that is within, and rested on the seventh day: wherefore I blessed the Sabbath and hallowed it." [Exod. 20:9-11].)

Blessed is the Creator of Nature Who sanctifies
all creatures by Your laws of Shabbat.

(For Saturday night: Blessed art Thou, Source of All Life, Creator of the light of fire, Who has distinguished between the sacred and the profane, between light and darkness. Blessed art Thou Who has created us so that we can distinguish brutality from kindness, mercy from mercilessness, good from evil, for if we could not make these distinctions darkness would cover the earth. Leader lights the havdalah candle and passes around the spice box so that all may smell its fragrance, and says: "This havdalah candle, braided with beauty, is a symbol of the intertwining of life. We bless Thee, God, Eternal and Majestic, Who did not create us in isolation but with a wonderful togetherness, and Who has given all Your creatures senses of enjoyment, to smell, to see, to taste, to touch, to hear, so that all creatures may know the wonders of Your world.)

U'RHATZ (Washing of the Hands)

הַדְלָקַת הַנֵּרוֹת

בָּרוּךְ אַתָּה יְיָ אֱלֹהֵינוּ מֶלֶךְ הָעוֹלָם אֲשֶׁר קִדְּשָׁנוּ בְּמִצְוֹתָיו וְצִוָּנוּ לְהַדְלִיק נֵר שֶׁל
(שַׁבָּת וְשֶׁל) יוֹם טוֹב

בְּהַלְלֵנוּ אֶת הָאֵל אָנוּ מְאַשְׁרִים אֶת קְדֻשַׁת הַחַיִּים בַּאֲשֶׁר הֵם.   נִחְיֶה עַל פִּי
חָכְמָה זוֹ, לְרַפֵּא וְלֹא לְהַזִּיק, לְהוֹקִיר וּלְקַדֵּשׁ, לְבָרֵךְ וְלֹא לְהִתְעַלֵּל, לִבְחֹר בְּחַיִּים לְמַעַן
כָּל מִי שֶׁהָאֵל הֶעֱנִיק לוֹ חַיִּים.

(בְּעֶרֶב שַׁבָּת אוֹמְרִים: זָכוֹר אֶת יוֹם הַשַּׁבָּת לְקַדְּשׁוֹ.   שֵׁשֶׁת יָמִים תַּעֲשֶׂה מַעֲשֶׂיךָ
וְיוֹם הַשְּׁבִיעִי שַׁבָּת לַייָ אֱלֹהֶיךָ.   תִּשְׁבֹּת לְמַעַן יָנוּחַ שׁוֹרְךָ וַחֲמֹרֶךָ (שמות כ"ג 12).   לֹא-
תַעֲשֶׂה כָל-מְלָאכָה אַתָּה וּבִנְךָ-וּבִתֶּךָ עַבְדְּךָ וַאֲמָתְךָ וּבְהֶמְתֶּךָ וְגֵרְךָ אֲשֶׁר בִּשְׁעָרֶיךָ; כִּי
שֵׁשֶׁת-יָמִים עָשָׂה יְיָ אֶת-הַשָּׁמַיִם וְאֶת-הָאָרֶץ, אֶת-הַיָּם וְאֶת-כָּל-אֲשֶׁר-בָּם וַיָּנַח בַּיּוֹם
הַשְּׁבִיעִי עַל-כֵּן בֵּרַךְ יְיָ אֶת יוֹם הַשַּׁבָּת וַיְקַדְּשֵׁהוּ.   (שמות כ' 11-10).)

בָּרוּךְ אַתָּה הַמְקַדֵּשׁ אֶת כָּל יְצוּרֶיךָ בְּחֻקֵּי הַשַּׁבָּת

(בְּמוֹצָאֵי שַׁבָּת אוֹמְרִים: בְּרוּכָה אַתְּ עֵין הַחַיִּים, בּוֹרֵאת מְאוֹרֵי הָאֵשׁ, הַמַּבְדִּילָה
בֵּין קֹדֶשׁ לְחוֹל, בֵּין אוֹר לְחשֶׁךְ.   בְּרוּכָה אַתְּ שֶׁבְּרָאת אוֹתָנוּ לְהַבְדִּיל בֵּין אַכְזָרִיּוֹת
לְרַחֲמִים, בֵּין חֶמְלָה לְקַשְׁיוּת-לֵב, אַתְּ שֶׁעֲדֶנָה שׁוֹרָה בְּכָל מַעֲשֵׂי יָדַיִךְ.   הַמְנַחָה מַדְלִיק(ה)
אֶת נֵר הַהַבְדָּלָה וּמַעֲבִיר(ה)   אֶת תֵּבַת הַבְּשָׂמִים בֵּין הַמְסֻבִּים שֶׁיָּרִיחוּ אֶת נִיחוֹחָהּ
וְאוֹמֵר(ת): נֵר הַהַבְדָּלָה זוֹ הַמִּסְלְסָל בְּיָפְיָהּ הִיא סֵמֶל לְנַתִּבוּלֵי הַחַיִּים.   נְבָרֵךְ אֶת הַבְּרִיאָה
הַנִּצְחִית וְהָאַדִּירָה עַל שֶׁלֹּא בְרָאַתְנוּ יְחִידִים. אַךְ בְּאַחְדוּת מֻפְלָאַת, וְעַל שֶׁלְּכָל יְצִירֶיךָ
הֶעֱנִיקָה   חוּשֵׁי תַּעֲנוּג לְהָרִיחַ, לִרְאוֹת, לִטְעוֹם, לְמֵשׁ, לִשְׁמֹעַ, לְמַעַן נֵדַע אֶת פִּלְאֵי
הַיְקוּם.)

וְרָחַץ (נְטִילַת יָדַיִם).   כֵּיוָן שֶׁהִנְּךָ מְקוֹר כָּל חֶסֶד וּצְדָקָה מִי יִתְּנֵנוּ וְנָבוֹא אֵלֶיךָ
בְּיָדַיִם טְהוֹרוֹת שֶׁלֹּא הֵזִיקוּ לְכָל יְצוּר שֶׁהוּא.

Because You are the fountain of all that is merciful and just, may we come to You with clean hands that hurt no creature.

KOS KIDDUSH: First cup of Wine: Sanctification of the Day

Baruch Atah Adonoi Eloheinu Melech ha-olam borei p'ri ha'gafen

Blessed art Thou, Source of All Life Who creates the fruits of the earth. We take up the Kiddush cup and proclaim the holiness of this Day of Deliverance from slavery.

Baruch Atah Adonoi Eloheinu Melech ha-olam sheh-heh-heh-yanu v'ki-y'manu v'higi-anu lazman hazeh

Blessed art Thou Who has kept us in life, Who has sustained us and brought us to this festival season. Amen. Let us now drink.

YAHATZ

This is the bread of affliction which our ancestors ate in the desert when they fled from Mitzrayim. This bread is the sign of pain. Yet by this bread we were saved in the desert and redeemed from our pain. By Your Saving Hand we were redeemed. In memory of our redemption from slavery, let all who yearn to be released from pain and oppression be released, let all who are in fear and terror be released, let their tears be wiped and their souls uplifted, let their hearts be consoled, and let Israel be Your messenger of this great redemption.

because you fed us and we were saved
we fled and You carried us on the wings of an eagle
by unleavened bread we became consecrated to You
by this bread we remember our enslavement
because we remember we seek the redemption of all creatures
from pain and human enslavement
Because You fed us with manna and we were saved
Let all who hunger be fed
Let all who suffer find mercy
And may we be the messengers of this redemption

Leader breaks the aphikomen and hides it.

Baruch Atah Adonoi Eloheinu Melech ha-olam ha-motzi asher kidshanu b'mitzvo-tav v'tzivanu al ahilat matzoh.

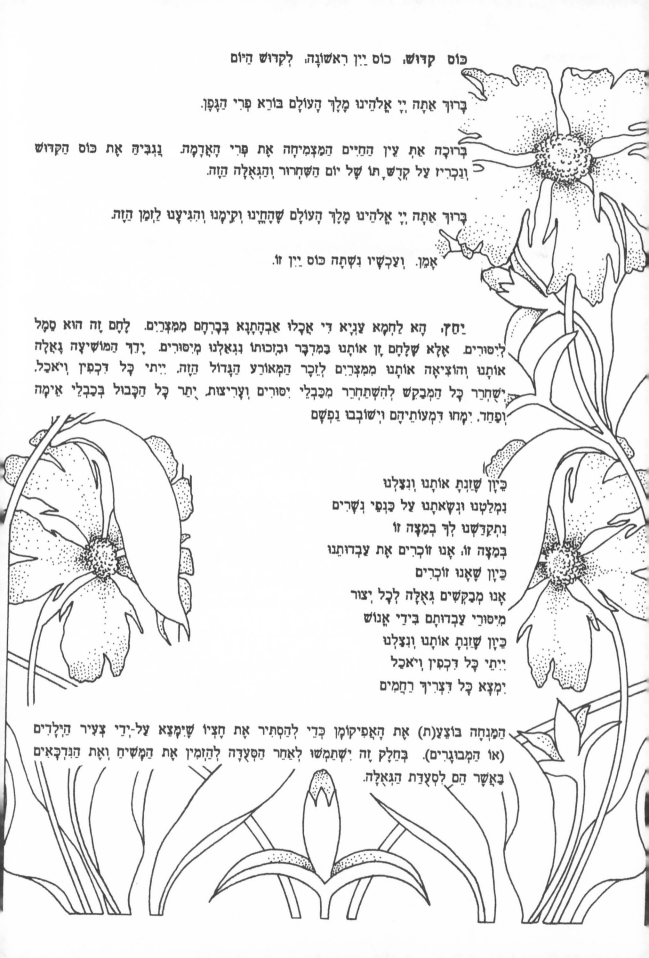

כּוֹס קָדוֹשׁ. כּוֹס יַיִן רִאשׁוֹנָה, לְקַדּוּשׁ הַיּוֹם

בָּרוּךְ אַתָּה יְיָ אֱלֹהֵינוּ מֶלֶךְ הָעוֹלָם בּוֹרֵא פְּרִי הַגָּפֶן.

בְּרוּכָה אֶת עֵין הַחַיִּים הַמַצְמִיחָה אֶת פְּרִי הָאֲדָמָה. נַגְבִּיהַּ אֶת כּוֹס הַקָּדוֹשׁ
וְנַכְרִיז עַל קְדֻשָּׁתוֹ שֶׁל יוֹם הַשִּׁחְרוּר וְהַגְּאֻלָּה הַזֶּה.

בָּרוּךְ אַתָּה יְיָ אֱלֹהֵינוּ מֶלֶךְ הָעוֹלָם שֶׁהֶחֱיָנוּ וְקִיְּמָנוּ וְהִגִּיעָנוּ לַזְּמַן הַזֶּה.

אָמֵן. וְעַכְשָׁיו נִשְׁתֶּה כּוֹס יַיִן זוֹ.

יַחַץ. הָא לַחְמָא עַנְיָא דִּי אֲכָלוּ אַבְהָתָנָא בְּבַרְהָם מִמִּצְרַיִם. לֶחֶם זֶה הוּא סֵמֶל
לִיסּוּרִים. אֶלָּא שֶׁלֶּחֶם זֶן אוֹתָנוּ בַּמִּדְבָּר וּבִזְכוּתוֹ נִגְאַלְנוּ מִיסּוּרִים. יַד הַמּוֹשִׁיעָה גָּאֲלָה
אוֹתָנוּ וְהוֹצִיאָה אוֹתָנוּ מִמִּצְרַיִם לְזֵכֶר הַמְּאֹרָע הַגָּדוֹל הַזֶּה. יֵיתֵי כָּל דִּכְפִין וְיֵאכַל.
יִשְׁתָּחֵר כָּל הַמְבַקֵּשׁ לְהִשְׁתַּחְרֵר מִכַּבְלֵי יִסּוּרִים וְעָרִיצוּת. יֵתַר כָּל הַכָּבוּל בְּכַבְלֵי אֵימָה
וָפַחַד. יִמָּחוּ דִמְעוֹתֵיהֶם וְיָשׁוּבוּ נַפְשָׁם

כֵּיוָן שֶׁזָּנַתְ אוֹתָנוּ וְנִצַּלְנוּ
נִמְלַטְנוּ וְנִשָּׂאתָנוּ עַל כַּנְפֵי נְשָׁרִים
נִתְקַדַּשְׁנוּ לָךְ בְּמַצָּה זוֹ
בְּמַצָּה זוֹ. אָנוּ זוֹכְרִים אֶת עַבְדוּתֵנוּ
כֵּיוָן שֶׁאָנוּ זוֹכְרִים
אָנוּ מְבַקְשִׁים גְּאֻלָּה לְכָל יְצוּר
מִיסּוּרֵי עַבְדוּתָם בִּידֵי אֱנוֹשׁ
כֵּיוָן שֶׁזָּנַתְ אוֹתָנוּ וְנִצַּלְנוּ
יֵיתֵי כָּל דִּכְפִין וְיֵאכַל
יִמָּצֵא כָּל דְּצָרִיךְ רַחֲמִים

הַמְנַחָה בּוֹצַעַ(ת) אֶת הָאֲפִיקוֹמָן כְּדֵי לְהַסְתִּיר אֶת חֶצְיוֹ שֶׁיִּמָּצֵא עַל־יְדֵי צְעִיר הַיְּלָדִים
(אוֹ הַמְבוּגָּרִים). בְּחֵלֶק זֶה יִשְׁתַּמְּשׁוּ לְאַחַר הַסְּעֻדָּה לְהַזְמִין אֶת הַמָּשִׁיחַ וְאֶת הַנִּדְכָּאִים
כַּאֲשֶׁר הֵם לִסְעֻדַּת הַגְּאֻלָּה.

Maror: Blessed art Thou Who hallows our lives with commandments. Blessed art Thou Who has commanded us regarding the eating of maror. (Pass bitter herbs on matzoh.) With these bitter herbs we remember our past oppressions. We remember all houses of bondage wherever mercy has fled and oppression and pain destroy God's world.

Charoshes: Blessed art Thou Who has preserved us to this day, on which we remember the mortar of slavery in Mitzrayim and the sweetness of life you give to those in freedom.

THE FOUR QUESTIONS and THE FOUR ANSWERS

Why is this night different from all other nights?

On all other nights we may eat leavened or unleavened bread, but on this night we eat only unleavened bread. Why is this so?

On all other nights we eat all kinds of herbs, but on this night we especially eat bitter herbs. Why is this so?

On all other nights we do not dip herbs at all, but on this night we dip herbs twice. Why is this so?

On all other nights we sit upright at the table. But on this night we recline. Why is this so?

We eat matzoh tonight in memory of our flight from Mitzrayim. We left in such haste that the dough in our ovens did not have time to rise, and when we came into the desert our bread was flat. The desert's sun baked our bread of freedom into flat bread.

We eat bitter herbs tonight because maror represents the bitterness of slavery.

Karpas: We dip greens twice, once to remember our past in Gan Eden as vegetarians and once to remember the future when we will be vegetarians again. We dip greens twice to bind the past and the future, remembrance and renewal. We also dip greens once in salt water to remember the bitterness of slavery. But we dip greens a second time in renewal of life and freedom.

We recline at the table because we eat at ease as free people, and not in alarm as on the night we fled Mitzrayim.

בָּרוּךְ אַתָּה יְיָ אֱלֹהֵינוּ מֶלֶךְ הָעוֹלָם אֲשֶׁר קִדְּשָׁנוּ בְּמִצְוֹתָיו וְצִוָּנוּ עַל אֲכִילַת מַצָּה

בָּרוּךְ אַתָּה הַמְּקַדֵּשׁ אֶת חַיֵּינוּ בְּמִצְוֹתָיו. בָּרוּךְ אַתָּה שֶׁצִּוָּנוּ עַל אֲכִילַת מַצָּה זוֹ
וּמָרוֹר. (מַעֲבִירִים אֶת הַמַּצָּה עִם הַמָּרוֹר). בְּמַצָּה זוֹ וּבְמָרוֹר אָנוּ זוֹכְרִים אֶת יְמֵי עֲנוּתֵנוּ.
אָנוּ זוֹכְרִים אֶת בֵּית עַבְדוּתֵנוּ. וְאֶת כָּל בָּתֵּי עֲבָדִים. כָּל מָקוֹם שֶׁנִּסְתַּתְּרוּ רַחֲמִים מִמֶּנּוּ. כָּל
מָקוֹם שֶׁבּוֹ הֶחֱרִיבוּ דְּכִי וּכְאֵב אֶת מַלְאֶכֶת יְיָ.

הַלַּיְלָה הַזֶּה אָנוּ אוֹכְלִים מָרוֹר

on this night we eat bitter herbs
because we were slaves in Mitzrayim
we have been abused, exiled,
the objects of experiments,
starved, beaten,
driven from our homes,
hunted, caged
our skins were used for ornaments

כֵּיוָן שֶׁעֲבָדִים הָיִינוּ בְּמִצְרַיִם

וְדֻכָּאנוּ

וְהָגְלֵינוּ

וְהָיִינוּ מָשְׂאֵי נִסּוּיִים

וְהֻרְעַבְנוּ

וְהֻכֵּינוּ

וְגֹרַשְׁנוּ מִבָּתֵּנוּ

Institutional cruelty does everything
it can to conceal the fact that it is
destroying its victims, and in doing
this it keeps its spectators from feeling
disgust and from being confused by the
paradox of trying to justify the unjustifiable,
of trying to praise the smashing of the weak.
Philip P. Hallie, *The Paradox of Cruelty*

וְנִרְדַּפְנוּ

וְנִכְלָאנוּ

וּבְעוֹרֵנוּ הִשְׁתַּמְּשׁוּ לְקִשּׁוּטִים

נֹאכַל מְרוֹרִים וְנִזְכֹּר

אַרְבַּע הַקֻּשְׁיוֹת

שֶׁבְּכָל הַלֵּילוֹת אָנוּ אוֹכְלִים חָמֵץ וּמַצָּה. הַלַּיְלָה הַזֶּה
כֻּלּוֹ מַצָּה. הַלַּיְלָה הַזֶּה אָנוּ אוֹכְלִים אֶת לֶחֶם הָעֹנִי.
לֶחֶם הַזִּכָּרוֹן וְהַגְּאֻלָּה. אָנוּ אוֹכְלִים מַצָּה זוֹ לְזֵכֶר עֲנוּתֵנוּ.
וּלְזֵכֶר יָדָהּ הַנְּטוּיָה שֶׁל הַבְּרִיאָה שֶׁגְּאָלַתְנוּ וְקִדְּשָׁה כָּל חַי בַּאֲשֶׁר הוּא.

שֶׁבְּכָל הַלֵּילוֹת אָנוּ אוֹכְלִים שְׁאָר יְרָקוֹת. הַלַּיְלָה הַזֶּה כֻּלּוֹ
מָרוֹר לְזֵכֶר עַבְדוּתֵנוּ. וּלְזֵכֶר בָּתֵּי הָעֲבָדוֹת הָרַבִּים שֶׁבָּהֶם חָיִינוּ.
לְזֵכֶר יִסּוּרֵינוּ הַקּוֹשְׁרִים אוֹתָנוּ אֶל יִסּוּרֵי כָּל נִדְכָּא.

שֶׁבְּכָל הַלֵּילוֹת אָנוּ אוֹכְלִים בְּלֹא דִין-וְחֶשְׁבּוֹן. אַךְ הַלַּיְלָה הַזֶּה
כֻּלָּנוּ מְסֻבִּים. כְּדֶרֶךְ בְּנֵי-חוֹרִין. וּמְסַפְּרִים אֶת סִפּוּר הַגְּאֻלָּה
וְדָנִים בְּמַשְׁמָעוּת הַבְּרִיאָה.

This is the Night of Vigil, when rabbis would sit until dawn and debate the miracle of redemption. It is customary to pose ethical questions on this night, and customary answers would be given by typical types of characters: the simple person, the uncaring person, the wicked person, the wise person.

The modern world suggests many questions which should be asked. Questions about slavery would be most appropriate for this occasion. The following poem was written by Paul Laurence Dunbar, son of two runaway slaves:

> I know what the caged bird feels, alas!
> when the sun is bright on the upland slopes;
> When the wind stirs soft through springing grass,
> and the river flows like a stream of glass;
> When the first bird sings and the first bud opes,
> And the faint perfume from its chalice steals--
> I know what the caged bird feels!

In his article, "The Life of His Beast," Rabbi Everett Gendler tells the story of Rabbi Zusya who traveled cross-country collecting money to ransom prisoners. He came to an inn at a time when the innkeeper was not at home. He went through the rooms, according to his custom, and in one of them saw a large cage with all kinds of birds in it. And Zusya saw that the caged creatures wanted to fly through the spaces of the world and be free birds again. He burned with pity for them and said to himself: "Here you are, Zusya, walking your feet off to ransom prisoners. But what greater ransoming of prisoners can there be than to free these birds from their prison?" Then he opened the cage and the birds flew out into freedom.

If slavery is defined as the commercialization of living creatures, the buying and selling of living flesh, can we describe animals in zoos, in cages, in slaughterhouses, and in laboratories as "enslaved"? Can you compare the conditions on slave ships with the conditions under which animals today are transported to slaughterhouses and laboratories. Keith Thomas pointed out in *Man and The Natural World* that the Portuguese used to mark slaves like sheep, with a hot branding iron. The historian, W.E.H. Lecky in his *History of European Morals,* compared the humaneness of Torah's law which states that we must not muzzle the ox when it treads out the grain in the fields with the condition of Sicilian peasants in the 18th century who worked in vineyards with their mouths muzzled so that they would not eat a single grape. Marjorie Spiegel's book, *The Dreaded Comparison:*

Human and Animal Slavery, explores the comparison between the two. Can you compare how animals are smuggled out of their natural habitats with the way that people are smuggled to be sold, how baby animals are separated from their mothers and often left to die with how the families of slaves are often separated in order to weaken their sense of their social bonds?

An appropriate question for children would be to comment on Maimonides' statement that "When it comes to the feelings of joy and sorrow that the parent feels for its young, there is no difference between the human race and animals."

We will hope that in these discussions, all children will be "wise" children.

We praise God, Sovereign of existence,
Lord of nature and of all life,
Guardian and Keeper,
Eternal Comforter and Shepherd
We praise You for Your bountiful munificence
You bestow life on all creatures
You called us for mitzvoth
You hallow our lives with commandments
You created us in Your image,
as merciful children of a Merciful Parent
You gave us the Shabbat as Your sign of the sanctity of creation
You gave us festivals for remembering and for rejoicing
With a Mighty Hand You brought us out of bondage again and
again
You preserved us to this day, and will preserve us forever.

How glorious is Your Name
Your dominion
Your creatures
Your laws
Your creation
Blessed art Thou Who has given us this joyful heritage
Who sanctifies us with Your image
And calls us to be merciful
Who sanctifies Israel,
Her festivals
And seasons of celebration
Your tender mercies are over all Your works,
and all the works of Your Hand praise You.

THE SECOND CUP OF WINE: Sanctification of Creation

Baruch Atah Adonoi Eloheinu Melech ha-olam borei
p'ri ha-gafen.

Blessed art Thou, Creator of the Universe, Who brings forth the
fruits of the earth. Blessed art Thou Who created the earth and
All that dwell therein.

Amen.

MAGGID

God brought Abraham from Ur to the Promised Land where he
dwelled with Sarah, and Hagar, his maidservant. Abraham had
two children: Ishmael by Hagar and Isaac by Sarah. Hagar was
sent away with Ishmael, where Ishmael became a mighty nation;
while Abraham continued to dwell in Canaan with Sarah and
Isaac. Then Isaac married Rebekah, who was chosen because she
showed mercy for animals. Abraham's servant went to Ur to find
a wife for Isaac. Having travelled for many miles through a hot
desert, he finally saw a group of young girls coming to a well for
water. He said to one of these girls:
"May I have something to drink?"
She responded:
"Drink, and I will also water your camel."

The servant was so taken by Rebekah's gentle response that he
chose her to be Isaac's wife and said,

"The maiden who has answered me thus
shall be the wife of my lord, Isaac."

Rebekah returned to Canaan with the servant,
and Isaac and Rebekah had twins: Jacob and Esau.
Though Esau was born first he was a hunter, and the blessing to
establish a mighty nation was given to Jacob.

Jacob had two wives, Leah and Rachel, and two handmaids:
Bilhah and Zilpah; and from them arose the tribes of Israel:
Reuben, Simeon, Levi, Judah, Issachar, Zebulun,
Dan, Naphtali, Gad, Asher, Joseph, Benjamin,
and a daughter named Dinah

Joseph's brothers were jealous of Joseph because he was talented
and charmed everyone and had been given a wonderful coat of
many colors, which was very rare in those days. His brothers did
a wicked thing and sold Joseph into slavery, and Joseph was

כּוֹס יַיִן שְׁנִיָה, קִדּוּשׁ הַבְּרִיאָה

בָּרוּךְ אַתָּה יְיָ אֱלֹהֵינוּ מֶלֶךְ הָעוֹלָם בּוֹרֵא פְּרִי הַגָּפֶן

בְּרוּכָה אַתְּ בְּרִיאָה נִצְחִית, הַמַּצְמִיחָה אֶת פֵּרוֹת הָאֲדָמָה. בָּרוּךְ אַתָּה הָרַחֲמָן,
שֶׁבָּרֵאתָ אֶת הָאָרֶץ וְאֶת כָּל שְׁכִנֶיהָ.

מַגִּיד

יְיָ הֵבִיא אֶת אַבְרָהָם אֶל הָאָרֶץ הַמֻּבְטַחַת,
וְאַבְרָהָם גָּר שָׁם עִם הָגָר וְשָׂרָה,
וְגִדֵּל אֶת זַרְעוֹ, יִשְׁמָעֵאל בֶּן-הָגָר, וְיִצְחָק בֶּן-שָׂרָה
וְיִצְחָק וְיַעֲקֹב, שָׂרָה, רִבְקָה, וְלֵאָה
גָּרוּ בְּאֶרֶץ כְּנַעַן וְשָׁם נִקְבְּרוּ.
וַיִּגְוַע וַיָּמָת אַבְרָהָם
וַיִּקְבְּרוּ אֹתוֹ יִצְחָק וְיִשְׁמָעֵאל בָּנָיו אֶל-מְעָרַת הַמַּכְפֵּלָה אֶל-שְׂדֵה עֶפְרֹן.
וַיְהִי אַחֲרֵי מוֹת אַבְרָהָם וַיְבָרֶךְ אֱלֹהִים אֶת יִצְחָק בְּנוֹ
וַיֵּשֶׁב יִצְחָק עִם-בְּאֵר לַחַי רֹאִי
וְאֵלֶּה שְׁנֵי חַיֵּי יִשְׁמָעֵאל מְאַת שָׁנָה וּשְׁלֹשִׁים שָׁנָה וְשֶׁבַע שָׁנִים,
וְהוּא בָּרַךְ בִּשְׁנֵים-עָשָׂר בָּנִים אֲשֶׁר שָׁכְנוּ מֵחֲוִילָה עַד-שׁוּר
אֲשֶׁר עַל-פְּנֵי מִצְרַיִם בֹּאֲכָה אַשּׁוּרָה

taken down into Egypt. But he was bright and soon won favor with Pharaoh: He became a trusted counsellor. At this time Pharaoh had very troubling dreams and asked Joseph if he could tell them what they meant.   Joseph believed that the dreams foretold of coming famine and he counselled Pharaoh to store and use his food supplies wisely. Thereby Egypt was saved from famine when the rest of the world lay covered with this doom.

> Famine was everywhere,
> famine, the precursor to disease and to slavery,
> raged everywhere except in Egypt
> because Joseph had counselled Pharaoh wisely

Even Joseph's father, Jacob, suffered and sent Joseph's brothers to Egypt to buy food. Joseph recognized his brothers and, though they had done him an evil deed, he forgave them and wept,
> "I am your brother, Joseph."

Even Pharaoh told Joseph to bring all his family to Egypt so that they could escape the famine that raged everywhere else, and so Jacob and all his childen and grandchildren, the tribes descended from Rachel went to Egypt, while the other tribes stayed in Canaan and waited for their return. But the Rachel tribes did not return for four hundred years. Jacob died in Egypt and asked Joseph to return his body to Canaan, to bury him in the cave in Machpelah, where Abraham and Sarah are buried.

> But they did not return for four hundred years.

First, Joseph's brothers prospered in Egypt and were glad to stay there. Joseph saw that he too was getting old and that the time for him to die was near. He made his brothers promise that they would return to Canaan.

> "You will surely return," he said to them.
> "When you do, carry my bones with you."
> Then Joseph died.

But his brothers and their descendants continued to stay in Egypt. Many years went by and one day there was a new Pharaoh who was not happy with all the Hebrews who had settled in his country. Little by little he made slaves out of them. Little by little, he passed one small act, then another small act, until all their freedom disappeared. Slaves are not always born slaves. Even people who have been free for centuries can lose their power and become enslaved. That is why Thomas Jefferson said that, "The price of freedom is eternal vigilance." One must never take freedom for granted.

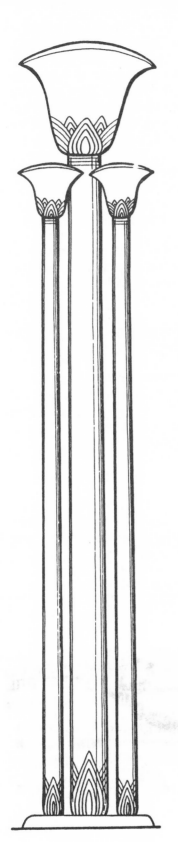

וּמִזֶּרַע יַעֲקֹב וְלֵאָה נוֹלְדוּ הַבָּנִים
רְאוּבֵן, שִׁמְעוֹן, לֵוִי, יְהוּדָה, יִשָּׂשכָר וּזְבֻלוּן.
וְאֶת הַבַּת דִּינָה טִימֵּא שְׁכֶם, וְאַחֶיהָ נָקְמוּ נִקְמָתָהּ.
וּמִזֶּרַע יַעֲקֹב וּבִלְהָה, אֲמַת רָחֵל, נוֹלְדוּ דָן וְנַפְתָּלִי,
מִזִּלְפָּה, אֲמַת לֵאָה, נוֹלְדוּ גָּד וְאָשֵׁר.
וּמֵרָחֵל אֲהֻבָתוֹ נוֹלַד יוֹסֵף בַּעַל הַחֲלוֹמוֹת
וּבִנְיָמִן, בֶּן-זְקוּנָיו.
אַף הוּא נוֹלַד מֵאֲהֻבָתוֹ רָחֵל.

וְיַעֲקֹב אָהַב אֶת יוֹסֵף מִכָּל בָּנָיו
וַתִּגְדַּל קִנְאַת אֲחֵי יוֹסֵף וַיִּמְכְּרוּהוּ לְעֶבֶד לְמִצְרַיִם.
וַיְהִי יוֹסֵף אִישׁ מַצְלִיחַ וַיִּשָּׂא חֵן בְּעֵינֵי פַּרְעֹה,
אֶת חֲלוֹמוֹתָיו פָּתַר וְיָעַץ לוֹ בְּחָכְמָה
וְנִצְּלָה מִצְרַיִם מֵרָעָב.
יוֹסֵף נָשָׂא חֵן בִּזְכוּת חָכְמָתוֹ וְהָיָה אִישׁ מַצְלִיחַ בְּמִצְרַיִם.

וְרָעָב הָיָה בְּכָל הָאָרֶץ,
רָעָב הַמַּכָּה הַהִיסְטוֹרִית כְּמוֹ
מִלְחָמָה וְעַבְדוּת, מַכּוֹת הִיסְטוֹרִיּוֹת
רָעָב הִכָּה בְּכָל הָאָרֶץ לְבַד מִמִּצְרַיִם
כִּי שָׁמַע פַּרְעֹה בַּעֲצַת יוֹסֵף.

וְגַם יַעֲקֹב סָבַל מִן הַבַּצֹּרֶת וְנִצְרַךְ לְשֶׁבֶר.
וּבָנָיו יָרְדוּ לְמִצְרַיִם וְלֹא יָדְעוּ כִּי חַי אֲחִיהֶם.
בָּאוּ לִשְׁבֹּר שֶׁבֶר וּמָצְאוּ
שַׂר וְשַׁלִּיט בַּחֲצַר פַּרְעֹה וְהוּא נָשָׂא קוֹלוֹ בִּבְכִי,
"אֲנִי יוֹסֵף אֲחִיכֶם."

וְהַקּוֹל נִשְׁמַע בְּבֵית פַּרְעֹה וַיֹּאמֶר פַּרְעֹה אֶל-יוֹסֵף,
"זֹאת עֲשׂוּ, קְחוּ-לָכֶם מֵאֶרֶץ מִצְרַיִם עֲגָלוֹת
לְטַפְּכֶם וְלִנְשֵׁיכֶם וּנְשָׂאתֶם אֶת-אֲבִיכֶם וּבָאתֶם."
וַיִּתֵּן לָהֶם מִכָּל טוּב אֶרֶץ מִצְרַיִם וְשִׁלְּחָם לְדַרְכָּם.

וַיַעֲקֹב בָּא, שֶׁבַע-יָמִים וְסִפְּקוֹ
"יוֹסֵף חַי", אָמְרוּ לוֹ בָּנָיו

Conditions became so bad for the Hebrew slaves, that Pharaohs arose who passed laws which required the death of Jewish male children. Pharaoh told two Hebrew midwives, Shiphrah and Puah: "When you deliver Hebrew women, if it is a boy, kill him, otherwise let it live." But the midwives refused to do this and secretly saved the male children. For this reason, our rabbis have said that "Israel was saved by women." The great modern female philosopher, Hannah Arendt, who fled the Nazis, once said that since nothing in human life is perfect, not even a totalitarian system can be perfect. It will have chinks and cracks and weak spots that even ordinary mortals can exploit. Thus we find heroic acts in every age, by all sorts of people, and under the cruelest and most extraordinary circumstances.

A woman named Jocheved bore a son whom she hid from Pharaoh for three months. No one exposed this deed. And one day she put this baby into a wicker basket, lined it with bitumen and pitch, and set it to float down the Nile River, hoping that the child would find someone who would take mercy on it and rescue it.

Which is just what happened

Throughout the ages parents have resorted to all sorts of tricks to rescue their children: They have put them on trains and on boats and into the hands of strangers so that the children could be taken out of an evil country to safety. Animals too will do anything they can to defend their young, even at the cost of their own lives. Wolves will risk gunfire from hunters to rescue orphaned wolves.

Pharaoh's daughter came down to the Nile to bathe. She was with her handmaids and slaves and heard a baby crying from the middle of the river. She knew immediately that "This must be a Hebrew child," and even though she was Pharaoh's daughter she rescued the baby and took him home and raised him in the palace.

And Moses was raised in the house of Pharaoh
like an Egyptian prince
He was raised in luxury and state power
and could have spent his whole life
as an Egyptian prince.
He had only one problem:
He was a stutterer
And could not be a flatterer

18

יַעֲקֹב שָׁמַע. אַךְ לֹא הֶאֱמִין. וַיִּסַּע לְמִצְרַיִם

וֵאלֹהִים קָרָא לְיַעֲקֹב-יִשְׂרָאֵל בַּלַּיְלָה

יַעֲקֹב. אָנֹכִי הָאֵל אֱלֹהֵי אָבִיךְ.

אַל-תִּירָא מֵרְדָה מִצְרַיְמָה,

כִּי לְגוֹי גָּדוֹל אֲשִׂימְךָ שָׁם.

אָנֹכִי אֵרֵד עִמְּךָ מִצְרַיְמָה,

וְאָנֹכִי אַעַלְךָ גַם-עָלֹה

וְיוֹסֵף יָשִׁית יָדוֹ עַל-עֵינֶיךָ.

וַיָּקָם יַעֲקֹב מִבְּאֵר-שָׁבַע וַיִּשְׂאוּ בְנֵי-יִשְׂרָאֵל

אֶת-יַעֲקֹב אֲבִיהֶם וְאֶת טַפָּם וְאֶת-נְשֵׁיהֶם בָּעֲגָלוֹת

אֲשֶׁר-שָׁלַח פַּרְעֹה לָשֵׂאת אֹתוֹ.

וַיָּבֹאוּ מִצְרַיְמָה יַעֲקֹב וְכָל-זַרְעוֹ אִתּוֹ

בָּנָיו וּבְנֵי בָנָיו אִתּוֹ בְּנֹתָיו וּבְנוֹת בָּנָיו

צֶאֱצָאֵי רָחֵל הָאֲהוּבָה וְכָל זַרְעוֹ הֵבִיא אִתּוֹ יַעֲקֹב-יִשְׂרָאֵל.

וְצֶאֱצָאֵי לֵאָה נִשְׁאֲרוּ בְּאֶרֶץ כְּנַעַן אַרְבַּע מֵאוֹת שָׁנָה וְחִכּוּ

וַיֶּאְסֹר יוֹסֵף מֶרְכַּבְתּוֹ וַיַּעַל לִקְרַאת-יִשְׂרָאֵל

אָבִיו גֹּשְׁנָה. וַיֵּשֶׁב

בְּאֶרֶץ גֹּשֶׁן וַיֵּאָחֲזוּ בָהּ וַיִּפְרוּ וַיִּרְבּוּ מְאֹד

בְּעוֹד רָעָב מַכֶּה בְּאֶרֶץ מוֹלַדְתָּם כְּנַעַן

וְאַחַר בָּא לְמִצְרַיִם וְהִכָּה בָּהּ

וְרַבִּים מָכְרוּ אֶת מִשְׁקָם וּמִשְׁכְּנוּ אֶת חֲרוּתָם

בַּעֲבוּר חִטָּה. מָכְרוּ אֶת יַלְדֵיהֶם לַעֲבָדִים

בַּעֲבוּר חִטָּה מָכְרוּ אֶת צְתִידָם

בָּאוּ לְמִצְרַיִם לִשְׁבּוֹר שֶׁבֶר רַב, וְהָיוּ לַעֲבָדִים

One day he saw an overseer, whose job it was to see that every
slave worked as hard as possible--he saw this overseer beating a
Hebrew slave and felt a terrible rage at such injustice. He could
not contain himself.   Horror at the sight of a man with a whip
beating a defenseless human being overwhelmed him and he
struck the overseer. The overseer died and Moses now had to flee
for his own life. He went into the land of Midian and joined the
tribe of Jethro, where he became a shepherd. Here he stayed for
many years, thinking about cruelty and injustice. He fell in love
with Jethro's daughter, Zipporah.   Slow of speech, he followed
the seasons and his own thoughts. One day when he was tending
the flocks, a lamb ran away for a very long distance. The lamb
ran and ran until it stopped at a little pool of water to drink.
Moses realized the lamb had run away because it was thirsty, and
that now it must be weary from its flight. He put the lamb on his
shoulders and carried it back to the flock, whereupon God said to
him:

You! Moses! I have chosen you
To lead my people Israel out of slavery
God chose Moses
as Abraham's servant chose Rebekah to be Isaac's wife
because they had shown mercy to animals

Then God led Moses to the burning bush and spoke:

Tell Pharaoh that the God of your ancestors
notes what is being done to My people
Tell Pharaoh: Israel is my firstborn
Let My people go that they may prepare a festival for Me
Tell Pharaoh: This is the earth My creation
I am that I Am
I Am Who Will Be With You Until the End
I Am the All-Present
I am Ehyeh and YHVH
I speak from the burning bush
that burns and is not consumed.

Tell Pharaoh: I am the Creator of all the world,
The Cushite, the Midianite, the Egyptian, the Babylonian
I am in the midst of all nations
as in the midst of this burning bush
Tell Pharaoh: Let My people go
That they may worship Me.

Then we rose with a clamor for our freedom
made plans in the night to flee.
Pharaoh said yes, then he said no.

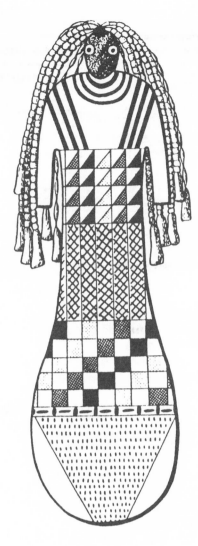

וַיָּקָם פַּרְעֹה אֲשֶׁר לֹא יָדַע אֶת־יוֹסֵף
וַיְצַו לְהָמִית אֶת בָּנֵינוּ הַזְּכָרִים,
כִּי חָשְׁשׁוּ פֶּן יָקוּם מִבֵּינֵיהֶם מָשִׁיחַ.
חֲשָׁשָׁם חַשַׁשׁ צָרִיצִים.
אַךְ הַנָּשִׁים הַמְיַלְּדוֹת רִמּוּ אֶת פַּרְעֹה,
הַנָּשִׁים. הַמְיַלְּדוֹת
רִמּוּ אֶת פַּרְעֹה
הֶחָלָב גָּאָה בְּחָזָן
לִשְׁמֹעַ בְּכִי הַתִּינוֹקוֹת שֶׁנִּגְזַר דִּינָם לָמוּת
וְהֵן רִמּוּ אֶת פַּרְעֹה וְהִסְתִּירוּ אוֹתָם.

וּפַרְעֹה אָמַר אֶל הַמְיַלְּדוֹת הָעִבְרִיּוֹת.
שֵׁם הָאַחַת שִׁפְרָה וְשֵׁם הַשֵּׁנִית פּוּעָה.
יַבִּילָדְכֶן אֶת־הָעִבְרִיּוֹת
וּרְאִיתֶן עַל־הָאָבְנַיִם אִם־בֵּן הוּא וַהֲמִתֶּן אֹתוֹ
וְאִם־בַּת הִיא וָחָיָה

וְיוֹכֶבֶד יָלְדָה בֵּן
וְעָשְׂתָה כְּכָל שֶׁיְּכֹלָה
וַתִּצְפְּנֵהוּ שְׁלֹשָׁה יְרָחִים
וַתִּקַּח־לוֹ תֵּבַת גֹּמֶא.
וַתַּחְמְרָה בַחֵמָר וּבַזָּפֶת
וַתָּשֶׂם בַּסּוּף עַל־שְׂפַת הַיְאֹר.
וַתִּתַּצַּב אֲחֹתוֹ. מִרְיָם. מֵרָחֹק. לְדֵעָה
מַה יֵּעָשֶׂה לְאָחִיהָ

וַתֵּרֶד בַּת־פַּרְעֹה לִרְחֹץ עַל־הַיְאֹר
וְנַעֲרֹתֶיהָ הֹלְכֹת עַל־יַד הַיְאֹר
וַתִּשְׁמַע בְּכִי מִבֵּין קְנֵי הַסּוּף
בְּכִי תִּינוֹק כְּצִיּוּץ הַצִּפּוֹר.
וַתַּחְמֹל עָלָיו וַיִּרְחַשׁ לִבָּהּ
בְּרַחַשׁ גָּדוֹל
וַתִּשְׁלַח אֶת־אֲמָתָהּ לַהֲבִיאוֹ מִן הַנָּהָר

Israel was saved because of righteous women:
an Egyptian, a Midianite, a Cushite, Zipporah,
midwives, Shiprah and Puah,
Miriam, the sister of Moses,
Jocheved, Deborah, Judith and Esther:
then and again in the Shoah
Hannah, Haviva, Vladka and Chaika,
Frumka, Zofia, Gisi, Niuta

Slaves were a luxury, but also a nuisance.
They could be rebellious, but they could be useful.
They were also his property. He felt he owned them.
Is this possible? For one person to "own" another?
To "own" another life? Can a living creature be property?
Well, Pharaoh said, "I own them!"
And hardened his heart against their cries
And worked them harder and fed them less,
And gave them straw to make their bricks with.

But God said: "You shall see what I shall do to Pharaoh,
He shall let you go because of a greater might
I am the Creator of all life, and I created all life in freedom.
And God sent terrible plagues to punish Pharaoh
because Pharaoh enslaved life and called it his property

THESE ARE THE PLAGUES GOD SENT:

BLOOD, BEASTS, HAIL, FROGS, BOILS,

LOCUTS, VERMIN, DARKNESS, PESTILENCE,

AND THE SMITING OF THE FIRSTBORN

Pharaoh relented.
He could not fight against this power.
He agreed to all the terms asked for

The night of liberation came.
We fled
The night of our redemption came
We fled with our families and tribes
A multitude of slaves with the shout
of freedom on our tongues

Even the dogs came to our aid
and barked at every Egyptian door
And led the angel of death away from ours

Our mouths were filled with the joy of freedom
Every nation said:
Great is their God
for see how they have been freed from slavery
Great is their God
For see how they go forth to build a nation
Great is their God

כְּשֶׁהָיָה מֹשֶׁה רוֹעֶה צֹאן שֶׁל יִתְרוֹ
בַּמִּדְבָּר. בָּרַח מִמֶּנּוּ גְּדִי אֶחָד וְרָץ אַחֲרָיו
עַד שֶׁהִגִּיעַ לְחָסוּת   כֵּיוָן שֶׁהִגִּיעַ לְחָסוּת
נִזְדַּמְּנָה לוֹ בְּרֵכָה שֶׁל מַיִם וְעָמַד הַגְּדִי לִשְׁתּוֹת.
כֵּיוָן שֶׁהִגִּיעַ מֹשֶׁה אֶצְלוֹ אָמַר לוֹ,
אֲנִי לֹא הָיִיתִי יוֹדֵעַ שֶׁרָץ הָיִיתָ מִפְּנֵי צָמָא, עָיֵף אָתָּה.
הִרְכִּיבוֹ עַל כְּתֵפוֹ וְהָיָה מְהַלֵּךְ.
אָמַר לוֹ הַקָּדוֹשׁ בָּרוּךְ הוּא,
יֵשׁ לְךָ רַחֲמִים לִנְהֹג צֹאנוֹ שֶׁל בָּשָׂר וָדָם כָּךְ.
חַיֶּיךָ. אַתָּה תִּרְעֶה אֶת צֹאנִי. וְהוֹבִילוֹ אֶל הַסְּנֶה הַבּוֹעֵר

הוֹבִילוֹ אֶל הַסְּנֶה הַבּוֹעֵר
כְּדֵי לְסַגְּלוֹ בְּמַרְאוֹת אֵשׁ
הוֹבִילוֹ אֶל הָהָר הַקָּדוֹשׁ
אֶל הַסְּנֶה הַבּוֹעֵר
אֶל הָאֲתַר הַמָּקוֹם

A woman can be a   great liberator.
In the 19th century, Harriet Tubman
Freed many slaves in the south.
Her people called her, "Moses."

There are more slaves
in the world today
than when the
Anti-Slavery Society
was established in the
early part of the 19th
century.   There is slavery
in Africa, Brazil,
the Dominican Republic,
Pakistan, Lebanon, many
parts of Southeast Asia and
parts of the Middle East.

This slavery consists
of selling women
and children into
forced marriages,
harems,
prostitution.
There is also
cruel child labor,
chattel labor,
debt slavery
and bond slavery.

הַגֵּד לְפַרְעֹה, יִשְׂרָאֵל הוּא בְּכוֹרִי
שַׁלַּח אֶת-עַמִּי לְמַעַן יַעַבְדֵנִי
שַׁלַּח אֶת-עַמִּי וְיָחֹגּוּ לִי בַּמִּדְבָּר
הַגֵּד לְפַרְעֹה, זֹאת הָאָרֶץ אֲשֶׁר בָּרָאתִי
אֶהְיֶה אֲשֶׁר אֶהְיֶה
אָנֹכִי הוּא שֶׁיִּהְיֶה עִמְּךָ לְעוֹלָם
אָנֹכִי הַהֹוֶה-תָּמִיד
אָנֹכִי אֶהְיֶה וְ-י-ה-ו-ה
אָנֹכִי סִבַּת כָּל דָּבָר
אֶשָּׂא דְּבָרַי מִן הַסְּנֶה הַבּוֹעֵר
אֲנִי הִנְנִי וְתָמִיד אֶהְיֶה
הִנְנִי וְאֶהְיֶה
דְּבָרַי מִן הַסְּנֶה הַבּוֹעֵר שֶׁאֵינֶנּוּ אֻכָּל

הַגֵּד לְפַרְעֹה, אָנֹכִי בּוֹרֵא הָעוֹלָם כֻּלּוֹ,
הַכּוּשִׁים, הַמְּדִינִים, הַמִּצְרִים, הַבַּבְלִים
אֲנִי בְּתוֹךְ כָּל הָאֻמּוֹת
כְּשֵׁם שֶׁהִנְנִי בְּתוֹכוֹ שֶׁל הַסְּנֶה הַבּוֹעֵר הַזֶּה
הַגֵּד לְפַרְעֹה, שַׁלַּח אֶת עַמִּי
לְמַעַן יַעַבְדֵנִי

Blessed be the Savior of Israel forever

By the banks of the sea
we sat down amazed
With a Mighty Hand You parted the waters for us
By the banks of the sea we sat amazed and trembled
for Pharaoh's armies came after us
We heard their chariots, heard their horses
but You parted the waters for us, and not for them.

How shall we sing of this wonderful deed?
How shall we remember this great salvation?
With laughter and with tambourines
With singing and with dancing
With worship and thanks and deeds of mercy

This is my God, whom I will enshrine forever
This is the God of my ancestors whom I will remember forever
Hei Haolamim

Creator of the Universe
Source of all Mercies
Return us
and we will return
to the Land of our ancestors

SANCTIFICATION OF ISRAEL: The Third Cup of Wine

Baruch Atah Adonoi Eloheinu Melech ha-olam
borei p'ri ha-gafen

Blessed art Thou, our God, Who created the fruit of the earth.
Blessed art Thou Who created the nations of the earth and Who
chose Israel from among them as Your firstborn

The Lord established for us laws in the desert
The Lord established us as a people in the desert
The Lord gave us our covenant in the desert
The Lord established the Festival of Freedom in the desert
Hag ha matzoh, the Festival of Unleavened Bread,
By which we remember our flight into freedom,
By which we remember all who are oppressed

The Lord fed us on matzoh and manna in the desert
The Lord brought us into the Promised Land from the desert
The Lord followed us by night in a pillar of smoke in the desert

דָם	צְפַרְדֵּעַ	כִּנִּים
עָרוֹב	דֶּבֶר	שְׁחִין
בָּרָד	אַרְבֶּה	חֹשֶׁךְ

וּמַכַּת בְּכוֹרוֹת

"הַנִּילוֹס מוּצָף הוּא, וְאֵין מִי שֶׁעוֹבֵד אֶת אַדְמָתוֹ. כִּי כָּל אֶחָד אוֹמֵר: אֵין אָנוּ
יוֹדְעִים מָה יֶאֱרַע בָּאָרֶץ" מֵתִים רַבִּים נִקְבָּרִים בַּנָּהָר שֶׁהָיָה לְקֶבֶר אָחִים וְהָיָה הַיְאוֹר
לְבֵית-הַחֲנִיטָה כֻּלוֹ דָם וְנִלְאוּ מִצְרַיִם לִשְׁתּוֹת מַיִם מִן הַיְאוֹר וַיָּצָא נַפְשָׁם לְמַיִם וְהַמִּדְבָּר
פָּשָׂה בְּכָל הָאָרֶץ בָּתִים נֶחֱרְבוּ וְשִׁבְטֵי פְּרָאִים פָּלְשׁוּ לְמִצְרַיִם הַשְׂחוֹק נֶעֱלַם רַק קוֹל קִינָה
נִשְׁמַע בָּאָרֶץ קִינָה וָנֶהִי (מִתּוֹךְ "תּוֹכַחַת אִפּוּוֶר". כְּתַב-יָד מִצְרִי הַמְבֻסָּס עַל כְּתַב-יָד מְקוֹרִי
מִשְׁנַת 2000 לפסה"נ לְעֵרֶךְ)

A chronicle from this time
documents catastrophes:
"The Nile is in flood, but no
one plows for himself, because
every man says: 'We do not know
what may happen throughout the
land.' Many dead are buried in the
river, the stream is a tomb and the
embalming place has become the stream,
the river is in blood. One cannot drink
from it and longs for water. The desert
has spread throughout the land, homes
are destroyed...only wailing is heard
in the land...."

בָּא לֵיל הַשִּׁחְרוּר
וְנִמְלַטְנוּ
בְּנִשֵּׁינוּ וּבְטַפֵּנוּ.
הָמוֹן עֲבָדִים נֶחֱרָדִים
וּלְכָל בְּנֵי יִשְׂרָאֵל לֹא יֶחֱרַץ כֶּלֶב לְשׁוֹנוֹ
כַּאֲשֶׁר עָבַר מַלְאַךְ הַמָּוֶת
בְּאֵימָה הִקְרַבְנוּ אֶת הַשֶּׂה
בְּעָבְדוּתֵנוּ הִקְרַבְנוּ בַּלַּיְלָה הַהוּא

וּבְחִפָּזוֹן גָּדוֹל יָצָאנוּ בָּאִישׁוֹן לַיְלָה
פִּינוּ נִמְלָא חַלְחָלָה

אָמוֹת אָמְרוּ:
אַדִּיר יְיָ
שֶׁגְּאָלָם מֵעַבְדוּת.
הַבִּיטוּ וּרְאוּ אֵיכָה הֵם צוֹעֲדִים!

Plague is as old as history, and references to it are
found in the writings of most peoples. It is humankind's
most global and most communal experience, involving in its sweep
more of humankind and nature than an earthquake, a tornado,
hurricane or a war. Where plague occurs, it eventually affects every
form of life, human and animal, and every institution. In the writings
of those who experienced plague in the past, the overwhelmingly repeated
sensation is apocalyptic. With all other diseases, however horrific
they are, human beings die singly, families mourn their own. In plague,
everyone is involved. Those who survive, survive as witnesses.

And gave us the cloud for a cover in the desert by day.

The Lord set the stars in the sky
And Israel upon their land,
created the lamb to know its mother,
the calf to know its field,
and Israel to know her God;
created the hen to guard her young,
the bird to build her nest
and Israel to be Your people.
God gave all life freedom and covenant
Set a table for us in the desert
where we ate the food of freedom, matzoh and manna

If You had done no more it would have been enough,
for who is like unto You, our God and our Redeemer

And yet! There were those who were not satisfied, complainers, naggers, the riffraff of little faith. Torah calls them "the murmurers." They complained and nagged because they did not have meat to eat and were willing to give up their freedom for meat. "Can God spread a feast in the desert?" they mocked. "Give us meat. Our gullets are shrivelled with manna. Give us meat to eat." A rebellion broke out in the camps, a food riot, because they were tired of manna. God became exceedingly angry with this display of gluttony and faintheartedness. Instead of lust for freedom, they lusted for the fleshpots of Egypt.

A wind from the Lord started up and swept quail from the sea, so much quail that the birds fell and fluttered all about the camp. The "murmurers" fell on the quail and for two days and two nights they gathered them up and stuffed their mouths and their bellies with the birds with such gluttony that the meat stuck between their teeth in unchewed lumps.

God's anger blazed out against the camp for this gluttony,
and the place, Kibroth-hattaavah, was struck with plague
because of the flesh eaters who were buried there

Time and again the people rebelled. Even Miriam rebelled against her brother because he had married a Cushite woman, Zipporah, black in color. She said to Aaron:

"Is Moses the only one who speaks for God?
Am I not a prophetess too?"

עַל גְּדוֹת הַיָּם
יָשַׁבְנוּ כְּחוֹלְמִים
בְּיָד חֲזָקָה בָּקַעְתָּ אֶת הַמַּיִם
עַל גְּדוֹת הַיָּם יָשַׁבְנוּ כְּחוֹלְמִים
רָעֲדָה נַפְשֵׁנוּ. כִּי הָיוּ אַחֲרֵינוּ חֵילוֹת הַמִּצְרִים
אֶת מַרְכְּבוֹתֵיהֶם שָׁמַעְנוּ
אֶת סוּסֵיהֶם שָׁמַעְנוּ
אֶת נִשְׁמָתָם הִרְגַּשְׁנוּ
וּבֶחָרְבָה נִמְלַטְנוּ מִפְּנֵיהֶם

נָשַׁפְתָּ בְרוּחֲךָ כִּסָּמוֹ יָם

אֵיךְ נָשִׁיר לְמַעֲשֶׂיךָ
אֵיךְ נִזְכֹּר יְשׁוּעָתֵנוּ
בִּשְׂחוֹק וּבְתֻפִּים
בְּשִׁירָה וּבִמְחוֹלוֹת

וַתִּקַּח מִרְיָם הַנְּבִיאָה אֲחוֹת אַהֲרֹן אֶת-הַתֹּף בְּיָדָהּ
וַתֵּצֶאןָ כָל-הַנָּשִׁים אַחֲרֶיהָ בְּתֻפִּים וּבִמְחֹלֹת.
יּשִׁירוּ לַיְיָ כִּי גָאֹה גָּאָה סוּס וְרֹכְבוֹ רָמָה בַיָּם."

סוּס וְרֹכְבוֹ רָמָה בַיָּם
בַּמִּדְבָּר הוֹצִיאָנוּ לַחָפְשִׁי
לַחֲגֹג חַג שֶׁל חֵרוּת
בְּמַצָּה וּבְמָן
הָרַחֲמָן הוּא כֹּחִי וְישׁוּעָתִי
הָרַחֲמָן הוּא אֱלֹהֵי אֲבֹתַי

חֵי הָעוֹלָמִים
אֲדוֹן עוֹלָם
בּוֹרֵא הָאָרֶץ
מְקוֹר הָרַחֲמִים
הֲשִׁיבֵנוּ
וְנָשׁוּב
אֶל אֶרֶץ אֲבוֹתֵינוּ

וְאֶת עַצְמוֹת יוֹסֵף לָקְחוּ עִמָּם.

God was angry with her for her criticism of Zipporah and
caused her to become sick with snow-white scales over her body.

Am I not the Lord of all nations? God said.
The Midianite, the Cushite, the Egyptian?

Moses wept for his rebellious sister
He wept for all his people
and pleaded with God to spare them

"If Thou must punish them,
let Thy wrath fall on me.
Though they be a sinful generation, preserve them
If Thou must punish them

let me die in their stead

Pardon, I pray, the iniquity of this people
according to Your great kindness
As You have forgiven them since Egypt

If Thou must punish them, take me in their stead"

Even after they betrayed him with the golden calf
when Aaron the mellifluous
inclined his ear to their requests
to build them a golden calf
while Moses was away on the mountain top
carving laws to make them into a just nation

he heard the shouts of idolatrous riot and broke the tablets
but returned and carved them again
for he would not let this people perish in ignorance:

I am the Lord your God Who brought you out of
the house of bondage
you shall have no other gods beside Me
you shall not make sculptured images, or any likeness
you shall not bow down to images and serve them
For I your Lord am an impassioned God
And will punish until the fourth generation those who reject Me
but will show kindness to the thousandth generation
to those who love Me and follow my commandments

You shall not swear falsely by the name of your God

נָתַתָּ לָנוּ חַיִּים בַּמִּדְבָּר

עָשִׂיתָ אוֹתָנוּ לְעַמְךָ בַּמִּדְבָּר

עָשִׂיתָ אוֹתָנוּ לְאֻמָּה בַּמִּדְבָּר

הוֹצֵאתָ אוֹתָנוּ כְּעַמְּךָ מִן הַמִּדְבָּר

כָּרַתָּ עִמָּנוּ בְּרִית בַּמִּדְבָּר

קִדַּשְׁתָּ לָנוּ חַג בַּמִּדְבָּר.

הֶאֱכַלְתָּ אוֹתָנוּ מָן וּמָצוֹת בַּמִּדְבָּר

הֶחֱזַרְתָּ אוֹתָנוּ לְאַרְצְךָ מִן הַמִּדְבָּר

לִוִּיתָ אוֹתָנוּ בַּלַּיְלָה עִם עַמּוּד הֶעָשָׁן בַּמִּדְבָּר

נָתַתָּ לָנוּ אֶת הֶעָנָן לְמַחֲסֶה בַּמִּדְבָּר

נָתַתָּ לָנוּ אֶת לֶחֶם הַחֵרוּת בַּמִּדְבָּר

אָכַלְנוּ וְנָטַשְׁנוּ אֶת עֲבוֹדַת הָאֱלִילִים

נָטַשְׁנוּ אֶת דַּרְכֵי הָעַבְדוּת וְאֶת עֲבוֹדַת הָאֱלִילִים

קָרְבַּן דָּמִים וַעֲבוֹדַת אֱלִילִים

כּוֹס שְׁלִישִׁית שֶׁל יַיִן, קְדוֹשׁ יִשְׂרָאֵל

הֵשַׂם אֶת הַכּוֹכָבִים בִּמְסִלּוֹתֵיהֶם.

הוֹשַׁבְתָּ אֶת יִשְׂרָאֵל אֶל אַדְמָתְךָ

בָּרָאתָ אֶת הַשֶּׂה שֶׁיֵּדַע אֶת אִמּוֹ.

וְאֶת הָעֵגֶל שֶׁיֵּדַע אֶת הַשָּׂדֶה

וְאֶת יִשְׂרָאֵל שֶׁיֵּדַע אֶת אֱלֹהָיו.

בָּרָאתָ אֶת הַתַּרְנְגֹלֶת שֶׁתִּשְׁמֹר עַל אֶפְרֹחֶיהָ

אֶת הַצִּפּוֹר שֶׁיִּבְנֶה אֶת קִנּוֹ

וְאֶת יִשְׂרָאֵל שֶׁיִּהְיֶה לְעַמְּךָ

נָתַתָּ לָנוּ חֵרוּת וְתוֹרָה

סִפַּקְתָּ אֶת כָּל צְרָכֵינוּ בַּמִּדְבָּר.

זַנְתָּ אוֹתָנוּ מִיָּדְךָ בְּמַצָּה וּמִן מִשָּׁמַיִם

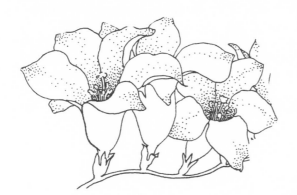

The first three chief rabbis of Israel
were vegetarians. Jewish vegetarians
exist throughout the world, in Australia,
Europe, England, and the United States.
There is an International Jewish Vegetarian
Society, which was founded by Philip L. Pick.
in London. Its headquarters are now in Jerusalem.

Some famous Jewish vegetarians are S.Y. Agnon,
Isaac Bashevis Singer, Franz Kafka, and Einstein

אִלּוּ עָשִׂיתָ אֶת כָּל זֹאת וְלֹא עוֹד - דַּיֵּנוּ

כִּי מִי כָמֹכָה בָּאֵלִים. הָרַחֲמָן

אַךְ הָעָם הֶחֵלּוּ מִתְאוֹנְנִים

הֲמוֹן קְטַנֵּי אֱמוּנָה וְחַסְרֵי לֵב

הִתְאַוּוּ תַּאֲוָה וַיֵּשְׁבוּ וַיִּבְכּוּ

וַיֹּאמְרוּ מִי יַאֲכִלֵנוּ בָּשָׂר.

"הַפּוֹרֵשׂ יְיָ סְעֻדָּה בַּמִּדְבָּר" לָעֵגּוּ.

"מִי יַאֲכִלֵנוּ בָּשָׂר כִּי טוֹב לָנוּ בְּמִצְרָיִם"

וְעַתָּה נַפְשֵׁנוּ יְבֵשָׁה אֵין כָּל בִּלְתִּי אֶל-הַמָּן עֵינֵינוּ.

תְּנָה-לָנוּ בָּשָׂר וְנֹאכְלֶהוּ (בְּמִדְבַּר י"א. 4. 6. 13)

וְהַמָּן כִּזְרַע-גַּד הוּא וְעֵינוֹ כְּעֵין הַבְּדֹלַח.
שָׁטוּ הָעָם וְלָקְטוּ וְטָחֲנוּ בָרֵחַיִם. אוֹ דָכוּ בַּמְּדֹכָה
וּבִשְּׁלוּ בַּפָּרוּר וְעָשׂוּ אֹתוֹ עֻגוֹת,
וְהָיָה טַעְמוֹ כְּטַעַם לְשַׁד הַשָּׁמֶן.
אַךְ הָאֲסַפְסוּף לֹא שָׂבַע נַפְשׁוֹ וּמְרִי פָרַץ בַּמַּחֲנֶה.
הָעָם רָצָה לְמַלֵּא אֶת קֻבָּתוֹ בְּבָשָׂר.
וְאֶת מַנְהִיגוּתוֹ שֶׁל מֹשֶׁה הֶעֱמִידוּ לְמִבְחָן זֶה:
הֲיוּכַל לְהַשְׂבִּיעַ רְצוֹנָם אִם לָאו. (בְּמִדְבָּר י"א, 7-8)

"מֵאַיִן לִי בָשָׂר לָתֵת לְכָל-הָעָם הַזֶּה,
כִּי-יִבְכּוּ עָלַי לֵאמֹר תְּנָה-לָּנוּ בָשָׂר וְנֹאכֵלָה.
חָרָה אַפָּם בִּי. כִּי אֶת תַּאֲוָתָם לֹא אוּכַל לְהַשְׂבִּיעַ."

וְרוּחַ נָסַע מֵאֵת יְיָ וַיָּגָז שַׂלְוִים מִן-הַיָּם.
וַיִּטֹּשׁ עַל-הַמַּחֲנֶה כְּדֶרֶךְ יוֹם כֹּה וּכְדֶרֶךְ יוֹם כֹּה
סְבִיבוֹת הַמַּחֲנֶה וּכְאַמָּתַיִם עַל פְּנֵי הָאָרֶץ.
וַיָּקָם הָעָם כָּל הַיּוֹם הַהוּא וְכָל הַלַּיְלָה וְכֹל יוֹם הַמָּחֳרָת
וַיַּאַסְפוּ אֶת-הַשְּׂלָו. הַמַּמְעִיט אָסַף עֲשָׂרָה חֳמָרִים
וַיִּשְׁטְחוּ לָהֶם שָׁטוֹחַ סְבִיבוֹת הַמַּחֲנֶה
הַבָּשָׂר עוֹדֶנּוּ בֵּין שִׁנֵּיהֶם. טֶרֶם יִכָּרֵת וְאַף יְיָ חָרָה בָעָם.
וַיַּךְ יְיָ בָּעָם מַכָּה רַבָּה מְאֹד
וַיִּקְרָא אֶת-שֵׁם-הַמָּקוֹם הַהוּא קִבְרוֹת הַתַּאֲוָה
כִּי-שָׁם קָבְרוּ אֶת-הָעָם הַמִּתְאַוִּים

בִּגְלַל אוֹתָם שֶׁבִּקְּשׁוּ לָשׁוּב
שֶׁהִתְאַוּוּ אֶל סִיר הַבָּשָׂר שֶׁל מִצְרַיִם.
שֶׁבָּחֲרוּ בְּגַרְגְּרָנוּת עַל פְּנֵי חֵרוּת

שׁוּב וָשׁוּב הֵם הִתְמַרְדוּ.
וַתִּשָּׂא כָל הָעֵדָה וַיִּתְּנוּ אֶת קוֹלָם וַיִּבְכּוּ
וַיִּלֹּנוּ כָּל בְּנֵי-יִשְׂרָאֵל עַל מֹשֶׁה וְאַהֲרֹן:
לוּ מַתְנוּ בְּאֶרֶץ מִצְרַיִם.
אוֹ בַּמִּדְבָּר הַזֶּה לוּ מָתְנוּ!
וְלָמָה יְיָ מֵבִיא אֹתָנוּ אֶל הָאָרֶץ הַזֹּאת
לִנְפֹּל בַּחֶרֶב
נָשֵׁינוּ וְטַפֵּנוּ יִהְיוּ לָבַז?
הֲלֹא טוֹב לָנוּ לָשׁוּב מִצְרָיְמָה."

Remember the Sabbath and keep it holy
Six days you shall labor and do all your work
but the seventh day is a Sabbath for the Lord your God:
you shall not do any work on this day,
neither you nor your sons nor your daughters
nor your cattle nor the stranger within your settlements

Honor your father and mother
that you may endure on the Land which I give you

you shall not murder
you shall not commit adultery
you shall not steal
you shall not bear false witness
you shall not covet

all who stand here before Me
Israelite, stranger, Hebrew and Midianite
with your families, your flocks, your cattle
you, beneath the vision delivered to me on the mountain
you are the Lord's forever

And the Lord said to Moses:
As you ask, so I pardon
But as I live and as My Presence fills the earth, My Creation
This generation who have seen My Presence
and the wonders I performed for them in Egypt
and in the wilderness
shall not see the Promised Land
Until the memory of lust and slavery wears away from them.
Forty years they shall wander in the desert.
The generation that enters the Promised Land shall have no
memory of slavery

Moses completed his work and died

The people inherited laws
And came to the Promised Land as a free nation

The Israelites marched on and encamped in the steppes of Moab, across the Jordan from Jericho. Balak, son of Zippor, saw all that Israel had done to the Amorites and he sent Balaam to prophesy against them. Balaam saddled his ass and departed with the Moabite officers, but the ass caught sight of the angel of the

אֲפִילוּ מִרְיָם קָמָה עַל אָחִיהָ,
עַל אוֹדוֹת הָאִשָּׁה הַכּוּשִׁית אֲשֶׁר לָקַח
צִפּוֹרָה, שְׁחוֹר עוֹרָהּ,
וַתֹּאמֶר אֶל אַהֲרֹן,
"הֲרַק אַךְ-בְּמֹשֶׁה דִּבֶּר יְיָ
הֲלֹא גַּם-בָּנוּ דִּבֵּר וַיִּשְׁמַע יְיָ."

יְיָ נָקַם בָּהּ עַל חַטָּאָה זוֹ.
וַתְּהִי מִרְיָם מְצֹרַעַת כַּשָּׁלֶג.
"הֲלֹא אֵל אֲנִי לְכָל הָאֻמּוֹת,
הַמְּדִינִים, הַכּוּשִׁים, הַמִּצְרִים."
אָמַר אֱלֹהִים, וְהִכָּה אוֹתָהּ בְּצָרַעַת

וּמֹשֶׁה בָּכָה עַל מִרְיָם הַמּוֹרָה,
אֲחוֹת יַלְדוּתוֹ הַמְּתוּקָה
שֶׁצָּפְבָה אַחַר גּוֹרָלוֹ
מִבֵּין קְנֵי הַסּוּף.
וַיִּצְעַק אֶל-יְיָ לֵאמֹר אֵל נָא רְפָא נָא לָהּ

בִּקֵּשׁ מֵאֱלֹהִים רַחֲמִים עַל יִשְׂרָאֵל
רָב עִם אֱלֹהִים
הִתְחַנֵּן לִפְנֵי הָאֱלֹהִים
לְכַפֵּר בַּעַד חַטַּאת יִשְׂרָאֵל.

"אָנָּא חָטָא הָעָם הַזֶּה חֲטָאָה גְדֹלָה
וַיַּעֲשׂוּ לָהֶם אֱלֹהֵי זָהָב.
וְעַתָּה אִם-תִּשָּׂא חַטָּאתָם וְאִם-אַיִן
מְחֵנִי נָא מִסִּפְרְךָ אֲשֶׁר כָּתָבְתָּ.
סְלַח-נָא לַעֲוֹן הָעָם הַזֶּה, כְּגֹדֶל חַסְדֶּךָ
וְכַאֲשֶׁר נָשָׂאתָ לָעָם הַזֶּה מִמִּצְרַיִם וְעַד הֵנָּה
שָׂא חַטָּאתָם וְאִם-לֹא מְחֵנִי נָא מִסִּפְרֶךָ.

גַּם לְאַחַר מַעֲשֵׂה עֵגֶל הַזָּהָב
כְּשֶׁשָּׂעָה אַהֲרֹן הַמָּתוֹק-כִּדְבַשׁ לְבַקָּשָׁתָם
שֶׁיַּנִּיחַ לָהֶם לַעֲבֹד אֶת עֵגֶל הַזָּהָב בְּעוֹד מֹשֶׁה עַל הַהָר
חוֹצֵב בְּאֶבֶן חֻקִּים
שָׁמַע אֶת קוֹל הֶהָמוֹן עוֹבְדֵי הָאֱלִילִים

Lord standing in the way and swerved aside into the field.
Balaam beat the animal to bring her back into the road, but the
angel of the Lord stationed himself again in such a way that the
ass had to squeeze herself against the wall. This caused Balaam's
foot to be squeezed too and he was furious that an animal should
cause him discomfort. He beat her again.

But again, too, the angel of the Lord moved forward so that the
ass had no room to move either right or left, and lay down in the
road and refused to move at all. Balaam became sick with rage at
the behavior of this animal and beat her until she was sore. But
God opened the ass's mouth so that she said to Balaam,

> "What have I done to you
> that you should beat me like this?
> Did I ever behave this way before?
> Have I not always done your bidding?"

> Then God uncovered Balaam's eyes
> And Balaam looked up and saw Israel encamped
> tribe by tribe
> and the spirit of God came upon him:

> Word of Balaam, son of Beor
> word
> of the man whose eye is true
> word of him who hears God's speech who beholds visions from
> the Almighty
> prostrate, but with eyes unveiled:
> How fair are your tents, O Jacob,
> your dwellings, O Israel
> like palm groves that stretch out
> like gardens beside a river
> like aloes planted by the Lord
> like cedars beside the water
> their boughs drip with moisture
> their roots have abundant water

> Their king shall rise above Agag,
> their kingdom shall be exalted
> Their God Who freed them from Egypt
> like the horns of a wild ox.
> They shall devour enemy nations,
> Crush their bones,
> Smash their arrows.
> They crouch and lie down like a lion.
> Who dares rouse them?
> Blessed are they who bless you

בּוֹגְדִים בַּעֲבוֹדָה שֶׁלֹּא נִשְׁלָמָה
וְנִפֵּץ אֶת לוּחוֹת הַבְּרִית אֶל לִבּוֹ

אַךְ שֵׁב, שׁוֹב וָשׁוֹב
שֵׁב, יוֹדֵעַ דְּבַר-מָה חָדָשׁ בְּכָל פַּעַם.
הַסַּכָּנָה שֶׁלְּעוֹלָם לֹא תֵעָלֵם
וְקוֹשֵׁר אֶת נִשְׁמָתוֹ בְּעֶצֶם הַזֶּה
מַטִּיחַ רְצוֹנוֹ כְּנֶגֶד רְסִיסוֹת-רוּחָם וּמוֹסֵר אֶת עַל חֲזוֹנוֹ.

אָנֹכִי יְיָ אֱלֹהֶיךָ אֲשֶׁר הוֹצֵאתִיךָ מֵאֶרֶץ מִצְרַיִם מִבֵּית עֲבָדִים
לֹא-יִהְיֶה לְךָ אֱלֹהִים אֲחֵרִים עַל-פָּנָי
לֹא תַעֲשֶׂה לְךָ פֶסֶל וְכָל תְּמוּנָה
לֹא תִשְׁתַּחֲוֶה לָהֶם וְלֹא תָעָבְדֵם
כִּי אָנֹכִי יְיָ אֱלֹהֶיךָ אֵל קַנָּא
פֹּקֵד עֲוֹן אָבֹת עַל-בָּנִים עַל-שִׁלֵּשִׁים וְעַל רִבֵּעִים לְשֹׂנְאָי
וְעֹשֶׂה חֶסֶד לַאֲלָפִים לְאֹהֲבַי וּלְשֹׁמְרֵי מִצְוֹתָי.
לֹא תִשָּׂא אֶת-שֵׁם יְיָ אֱלֹהֶיךָ לַשָּׁוְא
זָכוֹר אֶת-יוֹם הַשַּׁבָּת לְקַדְּשׁוֹ
שֵׁשֶׁת יָמִים תַּעֲבֹד וְעָשִׂיתָ כָּל-מְלַאכְתֶּךָ
וְיוֹם הַשְּׁבִיעִי שַׁבָּת לַייָ אֱלֹהֶיךָ
לֹא תַעֲשֶׂה כָל-מְלָאכָה
אַתָּה וּבִנְךָ-וּבִתֶּךָ עַבְדְּךָ וַאֲמָתְךָ
וּבְהֶמְתֶּךָ וְגֵרְךָ אֲשֶׁר בִּשְׁעָרֶיךָ.
כַּבֵּד אֶת אָבִיךָ וְאֶת אִמֶּךָ
לְמַעַן יַאֲרִכוּן יָמֶיךָ עַל הָאֲדָמָה אֲשֶׁר יְיָ אֱלֹהֶיךָ נֹתֵן לָךְ
לֹא תִרְצָח. לֹא תִנְאָף. לֹא תִגְנֹב
לֹא תַעֲנֶה בְרֵעֲךָ עֵד שָׁקֶר. לֹא תַחְמֹד

כָּל הָעוֹמְדִים לְפָנַי
יִשְׂרָאֵל, גֵּר, עִבְרִי וּמִדְיָנִי
עַל מִשְׁפְּחֹתֵיכֶם, צֹאנְכֶם וּבְקַרְכֶם
תַּחַת הַמַּרְאֶה בָּהָר הַזֶּה
לִי אַתֶּם לְעוֹלְמֵי-עוֹלָמִים

וַיֹּאמֶר יְיָ אֶל מֹשֶׁה סָלַחְתִּי כִּדְבָרֶךָ
וְאוּלָם חַי-אָנִי וְיִמָּלֵא כְבוֹד-יְיָ אֶת-כָּל-הָאָרֶץ
כִּי כָל-הָאֲנָשִׁים הָרֹאִים אֶת-כְּבֹדִי

and cursed are they who curse you

Because Balaam's ass saw the angel of the Lord,
Balaam prophesied.

Ninety-nine angels gathered together,
praised and exalted God and said:
Thy wholeness is marvellous
Thy kingdom is mighty
Thy wisdom is venerable

They trembled because of the majesty of God's voice, and said:
Thou art the Creator of Heaven and Earth,
Thou art the Just and the Living God
We exalt and praise Thy Name

They stood before God,
trembling and weeping bitterly
and asked for their food.

God said to the angels:
The clouds will bring your food in its season
and you will eat forever

The angels said to God:
What is Thy food, O Lord?
And God said to the angels:
My food is the praise of all creatures

The earth shouted and wept bitterly, and said:
I am always dry, give me rain, O Lord my Creator.
God heard the cry of the earth and said to the clouds:
Go and bring rain.
The clouds rose and went as God commanded them,
they ran and took the waters of God
to the place where God had sent them.
God drove a strong wind beneath the clouds to disperse them,
and said to the clouds:
Let the water go down.
They did as God commanded them.

Then the earth drank and was satisfied and blessed God:

Lord of the world Who gave me my food, the rain
I praise and glorify God

וְאֶת-אֹתֹתַי אֲשֶׁר-עָשִׂיתִי בְּמִצְרַיִם וּבַמִּדְבָּר.

וַיְנַסּוּ אֹתִי זֶה עֶשֶׂר פְּעָמִים. וְלֹא שָׁמְעוּ בְּקוֹלִי.

אִם-יִרְאוּ אֶת-הָאָרֶץ אֲשֶׁר נִשְׁבַּעְתִּי לַאֲבֹתָם:

אַרְבָּעִים שָׁנָה יֵלְכוּ בַּמִּדְבָּר

עַד יְמֻחֶה זִכְרוֹן תַּאֲוָתָם וְגִרְפּוּתָם.

אַרְבָּעִים שָׁנָה עַד יִפְּלוּ פִּגְרֵיהֶם בַּמִּדְבָּר

נָדוֹד יִנְדְּדוּ עַד יְמֻחֶה זֵכֶר עֲבְדוּתָם:

וְצֶאֱצָאֵיהֶם יִירְשׁוּ אֶת הָאָרֶץ אֲשֶׁר נִשְׁבַּע יְיָ לַאֲבֹתֵיכֶם.

הַדּוֹר אֲשֶׁר בְּחֵרוּת אָבְתָה נַפְשׁוֹ יִירַשׁ אֶת הָאָרֶץ

וְאָז כִּלָּה מֹשֶׁה אֶת מְלַאכְתּוֹ

יְיָ לְבַדּוֹ קָבַר אֶת מֹשֶׁה.

וַיִּסְעוּ בְּנֵי-יִשְׂרָאֵל וַיַּחֲנוּ בְּעַרְבוֹת מוֹאָב מֵעֵבֶר לְיַרְדֵּן יְרֵחוֹ. וַיַּרְא בָּלָק בֶּן-צִפּוֹר

אֵת כָּל-אֲשֶׁר-עָשָׂה יִשְׂרָאֵל לָאֱמֹרִי וַיִּשְׁלַח מַלְאָכִים אֶל-בִּלְעָם

לְמַעַן יָטִיל בָּהֶם קְלָלָה וַיָּקָם בִּלְעָם בַּבֹּקֶר וַיַּחֲבֹשׁ אֶת-אֲתֹנוֹ

וַיֵּלֶךְ עִם-שָׂרֵי מוֹאָב. וַתֵּרֶא הָאָתוֹן אֶת מַלְאַךְ יְיָ נִצָּב בַּדֶּרֶךְ

וַתֵּט הָאָתוֹן מִן-הַדֶּרֶךְ וַתֵּלֶךְ בַּשָּׂדֶה.

וַיַּךְ בִּלְעָם אֶת-הָאָתוֹן לְהַטֹּתָהּ הַדָּרֶךְ.

וַיַּעֲמֹד מַלְאַךְ יְיָ בְּמִשְׁעוֹל הַכְּרָמִים גָּדֵר מִזֶּה

וְגָדֵר מִזֶּה. וַתִּלָּחֵץ אֶל-הַקִּיר. וַתִּלְחַץ אֶת-רֶגֶל בִּלְעָם אֶל-הַקִּיר

Then the green grass and the trees of the plain appeared,
and all the birds of the sky and all the animals of the earth
Praised the Lord of Creation, the Lord of Redemption

THE FOURTH CUP OF WINE: The Cup of Redemption

Baruch Atah Adonoi Eloheinu Melech ha-olam borei p'ri ha-gafen

Blessed art Thou Who creates the fruit of the vine
Blessed art Thou Who redeems the earth Your creation
Blessed art Thou Who redeems Your creatures
Blessed art Thou Who redeems Israel
Blesed art Thou, Sustainer of the universe
We thank You for the fruits of the earth Your creation
We thank You for the bread of the earth Your creation
We thank you for the matzoh of redemption
We thank You for the manna of our souls
We thank you for seed and herb and fruit
for mercy, for life, for Torah, for covenant

Let us return to the garden of the Lord

I will extol Thee and bless Thy Name forever and ever
Great is the Creator, great is the Redeemer
Your greatness is unsearchable
One generation shall praise Thy works to the next
and declare Thy mighty acts as we do now
Let me think upon all Thy wondrous works
and speak of the might of Thy terrible acts.
I declare Thy greatness
I shall ever utter the memory of Thy great goodness
and sing of Thy righteousness forever and ever

Ha Shem has prepared a feast for us for this night
Manna and matzoh, honey, seeds and herbs
Hei Haolamim feeds us from the earth

All creation praises the Creator of the universe
the cows of the field gather together and sing
the cattle in Nineveh sing
"Sing, oh sing, acacia, tower in all your splendor,
you who are decked in golden embroidery
praised in the inmost sanctuary

the tabernacle of Hei Haolamim

וַיֹּסֶף לְהַכֹּתָהּ. וַיֹּסֶף מַלְאַךְ-יְיָ עֲבוֹר וַיַּעֲמֹד בְּמָקוֹם צָר
אֲשֶׁר אֵין-דֶּרֶךְ לִנְטוֹת יָמִין וּשְׂמֹאל.
וַתֵּרֶא הָאָתוֹן אֶת-מַלְאַךְ יְיָ וַתִּרְבַּץ תַּחַת בִּלְעָם וַיִּחַר-אַף בִּלְעָם
וַיַּךְ אֶת-הָאָתוֹן בַּמַּקֵּל. וַיִּפְתַּח יְיָ אֶת-פִּי הָאָתוֹן
וַתֹּאמֶר לְבִלְעָם, מֶה עָשִׂיתִי לְךָ כִּי הִכִּיתַנִי זֶה שָׁלֹשׁ רְגָלִים?
הֲלֹא אָנֹכִי אֲתֹנְךָ אֲשֶׁר-רָכַבְתָּ עָלַי מֵעוֹדְךָ עַד-הַיּוֹם הַזֶּה
הַהַסְכֵּן הִסְכַּנְתִּי לַעֲשׂוֹת לְךָ כֹּה? וַיְגַל אֶת-עֵינֵי בִלְעָם . . .

וַיִּשָּׂא בִלְעָם אֶת-עֵינָיו וַיַּרְא אֶת-יִשְׂרָאֵל שֹׁכֵן לִשְׁבָטָיו.
וַתְּהִי עָלָיו רוּחַ אֱלֹהִים.

נְאֻם בִּלְעָם בְּנוֹ בְעֹר וּנְאֻם הַגֶּבֶר שְׁתֻם הָעָיִן
נְאֻם שֹׁמֵעַ אִמְרֵי-אֵל אֲשֶׁר מַחֲזֵה שַׁדַּי יֶחֱזֶה
נֹפֵל וּגְלוּי עֵינָיִם.
מַה-טֹּבוּ אֹהָלֶיךָ יַעֲקֹב
מִשְׁכְּנֹתֶיךָ יִשְׂרָאֵל
כִּנְחָלִים נִטָּיוּ
כְּגַנֹּת עֲלֵי נָהָר
כַּאֲהָלִים נָטַע יְיָ
כַּאֲרָזִים עֲלֵי-מָיִם.
יִזַּל-מַיִם מִדָּלְיָו
וְזַרְעוֹ בְּמַיִם רַבִּים
וְיָרֹם מֵאֲגַג מַלְכּוֹ
וְתִנַּשֵּׂא מַלְכֻתוֹ.
אֵל מוֹצִיאוֹ מִמִּצְרַיִם
כְּתוֹעֲפֹת רְאֵם לוֹ
יֹאכַל גּוֹיִם צָרָיו
וְעַצְמֹתֵיהֶם יְגָרֵם
וְחִצָּיו יִמְחָץ.
כָּרַע שָׁכַב כַּאֲרִי
וּכְלָבִיא מִי יְקִימֶנּוּ
מְבָרְכֶיךָ בָרוּךְ וְאֹרְרֶיךָ אָרוּר.

What did I ever do to you that you beat me?
Numbers 22:21-34

There are probably no creatures who more
require the protective divine Word against
the presumption of man than the animals.
Rabbi Samson Raphael Hirsch

תִּשְׁעִים-וְתִשְׁעָה מַלְאָכִים הִתְכַּנְּסוּ יַחַד
פָּאֲרוּ וְהִלְלוּ אֶת אֱלֹהִים וְאָמְרוּ,
שְׁלֵמוּתְךָ מְסֻלָּאָה הִיא.
מַלְכוּתְךָ אַדִּירָה, חָכְמָתְךָ נַעֲרָצָה.

is made of the trunks of trees
birds sit in their branches and sing praises
the tabernacle of the Creator is drawn by oxen
see how they halt before the gates of Eden
the birds lift up their voices and sing praises
the cattle bend their knees before the gates of Eden

Blessed art Thou
Sovereign
Creator
Hei Haolamim
Ha Rahman
We thank You for the food of the earth
for the
matzoh of redemption
for the manna of the soul

I will extol Thee my God and Sovereign
I will bless Thy name forever and ever
Everyday I will bless Thee and praise Thee
Great is the Eternal and highly to be praised
Whose greatness is unsearchable;
One generation shall praise Thy works to the next
and declare Thy mighty acts.
Let me meditate upon Your works:
Others shall speak of the might of Your terrible acts,
But I will declare Your majesty.
Others shall utter the memory of Your great goodness
And sing of Your righteousness:
Our Creator is gracious and full of compassion,
Slow to anger and of great mercy,
Thy mercies are over all Thy works,
And all Thy works give thanks to Thee
and all Thy saints bless Thee.
One generation shall tell the next.
They shall speak of the glory of Thy everlasting kingdom
For only Your dominion endures forever.
You uphold all that fall
All who are bowed down with pain

The eyes of all the living wait upon Thee

Thou givest all creatures their food in due season
Thou, Thou openest Thy hand and they are satisfied

Thou art righteous in all Thy ways,
Gracious in all Thy works
Near to all who call for You

כּוֹס רְבִיעִית שֶׁל יַיִן   כּוֹס הַגְּאֻלָּה

בָּרוּךְ אַתָּה יְיָ אֱלֹהֵינוּ מֶלֶךְ הָעוֹלָם בּוֹרֵא פְּרִי הַגָּפֶן

בְּרוּכָה הַבְּרִיאָה, מַצְמִיחַת פְּרִי הַגָּפֶן
בְּרוּכָה אֵת הַגּוֹאֶלֶת אֶת הָאֲדָמָה שֶׁבָּרָאת
בְּרוּכָה הָרַחֲמָנִית הַמּוֹשִׁיעָה אֶת בְּרוּאַיִךְ
בְּרוּכָה אֵת הַנִּצְחִית הַקְּדוֹשָׁה וְהַנֶּאֱדָרֶת, הַמּוֹשִׁיעָה אֶת יִשְׂרָאֵל
בְּרוּכָה אֵת, עֵץ הַחַיִּים, שֶׁשִּׂמְחָתָה בְּחַיִּים

נוֹדֶךָ עַל פֵּרוֹת הָאֲדָמָה בְּרִיאָתֵךְ
נוֹדֶךָ עַל לֶחֶם הָאֲדָמָה בְּרִיאָתֵךְ
נוֹדֶךָ עַל מַצַּת הַגְּאוּלִים
נוֹדֶךָ עַל מַן נִשְׁמוֹתֵינוּ
נוֹדֶךָ עַל הַגַּרְגִּירִים וְהָעֲשָׂבִים וְהַפֵּרוֹת
עַל הַחֶסֶד, עַל הַחַיִּים, עַל הַגְּאֻלָּה, עַל הַתִּקְוָה

מִי יִתֵּן וְנָשׁוּב אֶל גַּנֵּךְ
מִי יִתֵּן וְנָשׁוּב אֶל בָּתֵּינוּ

חָלַף הַלַּיְלָה
מַלְאַךְ הַמָּוֶת הָלַךְ לוֹ
קוֹל צַעֲקַת הַתֹּהוּ, הַמַּבּוּל, קוֹלוֹת הַטּוֹבְעִים
הַחַיָּלוֹת כְּבָר אֵינָם
כָּאן בֵּיתֵנוּ בְּגַן הָעֵד
בּוֹאוּ עֵגֶל, שׁוּעָל, דֹּב, זְאֵב
פֶּרֶד וַחֲמוֹר, כֶּבֶשׂ, עֵז, שֶׂה
בּוֹאוּ אֶל מִשְׁכְּנוֹתֵיכֶם בְּגַן הָרַחֲמָן
בּוֹאוּ אָדָם וְחַוָּה אֶל גַּן הַבְּרִיאָה
קִצְרוּ אֶת הַדָּגָן שֶׁנִּזְרַע בְּשַׁחַר הַבְּרִיאָה

הַשֵּׁם הֵכִין לְמַעֲנֵנוּ סְעֻדָּה
מִן וּמַצּוֹת, דְּבַשׁ, זַרְעוֹנִים, יָרָק
חֵי הָעוֹלָמִים מְזִינֵנוּ מִן הָאֲדָמָה
בּוֹאוּ יוֹנָה, זַרְזִיר, דָּג, קוֹף, בַּבּוּן וְשִׁימְפַּנְזָה
לֵיל הַחֲשֵׁכָה חָלַף, אֵין מִי שֶׁיַּחֲרִידְכֶם עוֹד
בּוֹאִי אֲתוֹנוֹ שֶׁל בִּלְעָם הַנְּחוּתָה שֶׁבַּחַיּוֹת

You fulfill the desire of them that fear You
You hear their cry and save them
You preserve all who love You
but the wicked shall be destroyed

My mouth shall speak Your praise
And all living flesh bless Your Holy Name

Arise, the winter is over
and the voice of the turtle dove is heard in the land

winter is past and flowers appear on the earth
the time of singing is here
My love turns to me and I to my love
Who leads the flock to feed among the flowers

Hei Haolamim set the stars in the skies
Hei Haolamim set Israel upon Her Land
Hei Haolamim set the creatures upon the earth
Hei Haolamim marked off the waters from the hills
Hei Haolamim shaped each creature with genius
each lamb to know its mother
each calf to know its field
each hen to guard her nest
each bird to feed its young
and Israel to know Your Presence

turn, turn, and turn again
we return like her young to the hen
suckled by You
sheltered by You
fed by You
guided by You

arise, sheep, lamb, goats, cattle
gather at the tree of life
for our God has brought us into a good Land
a Land with streams and springs and fountains
a Land of wheat and barley
of vines, figs, pomegranates, of olive trees and honey
These are the seven foods of the Land of justice
Where we may eat generously and fear nothing

To those who wait in the diaspora, we say:
Next year in Jerusalem

To Hagar and to Sarah
Return to the garden of life

שְׂאִי אֶת הַמָּשִׁיחַ וּבוֹא
לִוְיָתָן וּבְהֵמוֹת
עוֹרֵב שֶׁל נֹחַ, אַיָּלָה וַחֲמוֹר
בּוֹאוּ שָׁמִיר, תּוֹלַעַת, הַלְלוּ
הַלֵּל וְנִכָּנְסוּ לְעֵדֶן מֵאֲחוֹרֵי שַׁעַר הַבְּרִיאָת.

רְאוּ כֵּיצַד הוּא נִשָּׂא עַל גַּבּוֹת שְׁוָרִים,
הַבְּרִיאָה כֻּלָּה תְּהַלֵּל אֶת בּוֹרֵא-עוֹלָם
הַפָּרוֹת בָּאֲחוּ יִתְכַּנְּסוּ וְיִתְּנוּ קוֹלָן בְּשִׁיר
הַפָּרוֹת שֶׁנִּצְּלוּ בְּנִיגּוֹנָה שָׁרוּ
"רְנִי, רָנִי הַשִּׁטָּה!
הִתְנוֹפְפִי בְּרֹב הֲדָרֵךְ-
הַמְחֻשָּׁקֶת בְּרִקְמֵי-זָהָב
הַמְהֻלָּלָה בִּדְבִיר-אַרְמוֹן,
הַמְפֹאָרָה בַּעֲדִי-עֲדָיִים."

סֻכָּתוֹ שֶׁל חֵי הָעוֹלָמִים
בְּנוּיָה גִּזְעֵי עֵצִים
צִפּוֹרִים יוֹשְׁבוֹת עַל עֲנָפֵיהֶם וְשָׁרוֹת שִׁירֵי תְהִלָּה
סֻכָּתוֹ שֶׁל הַבּוֹרֵא נִשָּׂאת עַל כִּתְפֵי שְׁוָרִים
רְאוּ כֵּיצַד הֵם נֶעֱצָרִים בְּפַתְחֵשׁאַרֵי עֵדֶן

בָּרוּךְ אַתָּה
רִבּוֹן
בּוֹרֵא
חֵי הָעוֹלָמִים
הָרַחֲמָן
נוֹדֶךְ עַל מָזוֹן הָאֲדָמָה
עַל מֶצַת הַגְּאֻלָּה
עַל מָן הַגֶּשֶׁם
עַל גַּרְגִּיר וְיֶרֶק וּפְרִי

כָּל הַלַּיְלָה יָשְׁבוּ רַבִּי עֲקִיבָא וּבֶן עַזַּאי וְדָנוּ בָּשׁ אֵלָּה אֵיזֶהוּ הַפָּסוּק הַמַּכְרִיז
עַל הָעִקָּר הֶחָשׁוּב בְּיוֹתֵר בַּתּוֹרָה. כָּל הַלַּיְלָה יָשַׁבְנוּ מִסָּבִיב לַשׁ לְחָן
וְהִקְשַׁבְנוּ לְוִכּוּחָם. רַבִּי עֲקִיבָא אָמַר, "וְאָהַבְתָּ לְרֵעֲךָ כָּמוֹךָ (וַיִּקְרָא י"ט, 18).
הוּא עִקָּר-הָעִקָּרִים, כִּי מַה שֶּׁשָּׂנוּא עָלֶיךָ, לֹא תַּעֲשֶׂה לַחֲבֵרְךָ. מְסִלַּת יְשָׁרִים.
לֵךְ בַּדֶּרֶךְ הַיָּשָׁר:

and build new homes with unguarded lintels

Baruch Atah Adonoi Eloheinu Melech ha-olam ha-motzi lehem min ha-aretz

Blessed art Thou Who gives us our food from the earth. Amen

(On Shabbat, add: May we inherit a day which will be Shabbat for eternity.)

THE MEAL IS SERVED

Grace: Gather at an open door with the aphikomen and the Cup of Elijah and say:

Praise the Living God from Whose bounty we have fed and by
Whose goodness we live, through Whose compassion all
existence is sustained, and Whose surpassing goodness fills all
time and space. (Share the aphikomen and throw matzoh outdoors
and say)

I call heaven and earth to be my witness
that the Holy One
sits and divides provisions
among all who come into the world
from human to animal to creeping thing,
to the bird in the sky.
Let all who hunger be fed on this night
Let every creature who is in pain be redeemed on this night.

Chalutzim of the Messiah: Let us gather at this door and recognize that the source of our spiritual life and our vision of the future are one: "The free movement of the moral impulse to establish justice for animals generally and the claim of their rights from mankind are hidden in a moral psychic sensibility in the deeper layers of the Torah: I have given you every herb yielding seed and all the fruit of a tree yielding seed for food. Is it therefore possible to conceive that a virtue of such priceless value, which had at one time been a possession of humankind, should be lost forever? (Rabbi Yitzchak HaCohen Kuk)

Let us give thanks to our Creator
Who performs great marvels,
who made the heavens and the earth
Who spread out the earth above the waters
Who made the lights in the heavens:
The sun to rule by day and the moon to rule by night;

רַבִּי בֶּן עַזַאי אָמַר: "עִקַּר-הָעִקָּרִים נִקְבַּע בְּבְּרֵאשִׁית ה' 1.
זֶה סֵפֶר תּוֹלְדוֹת אָדָם בְּיוֹם בְּרֹא אֱלֹהִים אָדָם
בִּדְמוּת אֱלֹהִים עָשָׂה אֹתוֹ:"

"וַהֲרֵי זֶה מוֹכִיחַ אֶת עֶקְרוֹנִי:" אָמַר רַבִּי עֲקִיבָא. "אֲנַחְנוּ
יַלְדֵי חַסְדּוֹ שֶׁל אֵל רַב-חָסֶד. דַּעַת תְּבוּנוֹת בָּרֵי לֵב יֹדַעַ:"

"רַבֵּנוּ:" שָׁאֲלוּ תַלְמִידָיו, "אֵיזֶהוּ עִקָּר גָּדוֹל יוֹתֵר,
צַעַר בַּעֲלֵי חַיִּים אוֹ עֵרֶךְ הַמִּין הָאֱנוֹשִׁי שֶׁנַּעֲשָׂה
בִּדְמוּתוֹ שֶׁל הָאֱלֹהִים?"

"צַעַר בַּעֲלֵי חַיִּים:" אָמַר לָהֶם. "שֶׁאִם נִשְׁכַּח עִקָּר זֶה לֹא עוֹד נִהְיֶה בִּדְמוּתוֹ שֶׁל אֱלֹהִים. דֶּרֶךְ
הַשֵּׁם, דַּרְכּוֹ שֶׁל אֱלֹהִים, רַחֲמָנִים בְּנֵי רַחֲמָנִים."

וְאָז שָׂר הָרוֹעֶה-הָרַב עִם תַּלְמִידָיו:

אֲרוֹמִמְךָ אֱלוֹהַי הַמֶּלֶךְ וַאֲבָרְכָה שִׁמְךָ לְעוֹלָם וָעֶד
בְּכָל-יוֹם אֲבָרְכֶךָּ וַאֲהַלְלָה שִׁמְךָ לְעוֹלָם וָעֶד
גָּדוֹל יְיָ וּמְהֻלָּל מְאֹד וְלִגְדֻלָּתוֹ אֵין חֵקֶר;
דּוֹר לְדוֹר יְשַׁבַּח מַעֲשֶׂיךָ וּגְבוּרֹתֶיךָ יַגִּידוּ.
הֲדַר כְּבוֹד הוֹדֶךָ וְדִבְרֵי נִפְלְאֹתֶיךָ אָשִׂיחָה.
וֶעֱזוּז נוֹרְאֹתֶיךָ יֹאמֵרוּ וּגְדוּלָּתְךָ אֲסַפְּרֶנָּה;
זֵכֶר רַב-טוּבְךָ יַבִּיעוּ וְצִדְקָתְךָ יְרַנֵּנוּ,
חַנּוּן וְרַחוּם יְיָ אֶרֶךְ אַפַּיִם וּגְדָל-חָסֶד.
טוֹב יְיָ לַכֹּל וְרַחֲמָיו עַל-כָּל-מַעֲשָׂיו.
יוֹדוּךָ יְיָ כָּל-מַעֲשֶׂיךָ וַחֲסִידֶיךָ יְבָרְכוּכָה.
כְּבוֹד מַלְכוּתְךָ יֹאמֵרוּ וּגְבוּרָתְךָ יְדַבֵּרוּ
לְהוֹדִיעַ לִבְנֵי הָאָדָם גְּבוּרֹתָיו וּכְבוֹד הֲדַר מַלְכוּתוֹ.
מַלְכוּתְךָ מַלְכוּת כָּל-עֹלָמִים וּמֶמְשַׁלְתְּךָ בְּכָל-דּוֹר וָדֹר.
סוֹמֵךְ יְיָ לְכָל-הַנֹּפְלִים וְזוֹקֵף לְכָל-הַכְּפוּפִים
עֵינֵי כֹל אֵלֶיךָ יְשַׂבֵּרוּ

Who smote Pharaoh and brought Israel out of slavery
With a Strong Hand and an Outstretched Arm,
Who parted the Sea of Reeds
And allowed Israel to pass through in safety.
Who overthrew Pharaoh in the midst of its waters
Who led Israel through the wilderness
Who smote great kings, Sihon king of the Amorites
and Og, king of Bashan
Who gave the Promised Land for a heritage to Israel;
Who remembers us in our low estate
and releases us from our adversaries

You it is Who feeds all Your creatures
Give thanks to the God of Heaven
and return us, God, return us to Your garden
Amen

Thou art very great
Thou art clothed with honor and majesty
With light as with a garment
You stretched out the heavens like a curtain
You laid the beams of Your creation in the waters
The clouds are Your chariot
You walk upon the wings of the wind
The winds are Your messengers
Your ministers are a flaming fire

You laid the foundations of the earth for all eternity
You covered it with waters as with a vesture
The waters stood above the mountains
At Your command they fled past the mountains
and down into the valleys
You set boundaries about them
so that they may not flood the earth again

You send forth springs into the valleys
They run among the mountains
They quench the thirst of beasts in the field
The wild asses quench their thirst
And the fowl have their habitation there
They sing among the branches
You water the mountains from Your heavens
The earth is satisfied with the fruit of Your works
You cause the grass to grow for the cattle
And give herbs for us to eat
So that we may bring forth our food from the earth
Wine to make us glad
Oil to make our faces shine

וְאַתָּה נוֹתֵן-לָהֶם אֶת-אָכְלָם בְּעִתּוֹ
פּוֹתֵחַ אֶת-יָדֶךָ וּמַשְׂבִּיעַ לְכָל-חַי רָצוֹן

צַדִּיק יְיָ בְּכָל-דְּרָכָיו וְחָסִיד בְּכָל מַעֲשָׂיו
קָרוֹב יְיָ לְכָל קֹרְאָיו לְכֹל אֲשֶׁר יִקְרָאֻהוּ בֶאֱמֶת
רְצוֹן-יְרֵאָיו יַעֲשֶׂה וְאֶת שַׁוְעָתָם יִשְׁמַע וְיוֹשִׁיעֵם
שׁוֹמֵר יְיָ אֶת-כָּל-אֹהֲבָיו וְאֵת כָּל הָרְשָׁעִים יַשְׁמִיד
תְּהִלַּת יְיָ יְדַבֶּר-פִּי וִיבָרֵךְ כָּל-בָּשָׂר שֵׁם קָדְשׁוֹ לְעוֹלָם וָעֶד.

קוּמִי לָךְ
כִּי-הִנֵּה הַלַּיְלָה עָבָר
הַגֶּשֶׁם חָלַף הָלַךְ לוֹ
בָּאָה עוֹנַת הַקָּצִיר הָאָבִיב הִגִּיעַ
בָּאָה חִטָּה
קוּמִי לָכְי רַעְיָתִי יָסָתִי
וּלְכִי-לָךְ

כִּי-הִנֵּה הַחֹרֶף עָבָר הַגְּשָׁמִים נִרְאוּ בָאָרֶץ
עֵת הַזָּמִיר הִגִּיעַ
וְקוֹל הַתּוֹר נִשְׁמַע בְּאַרְצֵנוּ
דּוֹדִי לִי וַאֲנִי לוֹ.
הָרֹעֶה בַּשּׁוֹשַׁנִּים

חֵי הָעוֹלָמִים שָׂם אֶת הַכּוֹכָבִים בִּמְסִלּוֹתֵיהֶם
חֵי הָעוֹלָמִים שָׂם אֶת יִשְׂרָאֵל עַל אַדְמָתוֹ
חֵי הָעוֹלָמִים שָׂם אֶת בְּרוּאָיו עַל הָאָרֶץ
חֵי הָעוֹלָמִים הִפְרִיד יַמִּים מִגְּבָעוֹת
חֵי הָעוֹלָמִים עִצֵּב כָּל יְצוּר בִּגְאוֹנוֹת
כָּל שֶׂה שֶׁיֵּדַע אֶת אִמּוֹ
כָּל עֵגֶל שֶׁיֵּדַע אֶת שָׂדֶה מִרְעֵהוּ
כָּל תַּרְנְגֹלֶת שֶׁתָּגֵן עַל קִנָּהּ
כָּל צִפּוֹר שֶׁתַּאֲכִיל אֶת גּוֹזָלֶיהָ
וְיִשְׂרָאֵל שֶׁיֵּדַע הֱיוֹתֵךְ

Bread to make us strong

Your trees are satisfied with Your design
The cedars of Lebanon which You planted
where birds make their nests and storks make their homes
The high mountains are for the wild goats
and the rocks are a refuge for the conies

You appointed the moon for seasons
The sun to know its path:
You make darkness and it is night
when all the beasts of the forest go forth
The young lions roar for their food, and seek it from You
The sun rises, they go away and lay down in their dens
We go forth to work to our labor until the evening

How manifold are Your works
In wisdom You made them all
The whole earth is full of Your riches:
Yonder is the sea, great and wide,
filled with fish and creeping animals, small and great,
there go the ships;
There is Leviathan whom You made to play in the waters:
all these wait upon You
That You may give them their food in due season

You open Your Hand
They are satisfied
You hide Your face
They are troubled
You take away their breath
They die and return to dust
You send forth Your spirit, they are created:
You renew the face of the ground

Return us, Sovereign of Life
Return us to Your garden

Amen

סֹב, סֹב וְשׁוֹב נָסֹב
כְּאֶפְרֹחֵי הַתַּרְנְגֹלֶת נָשׁוּב
אֶת מְנִיקָתֵנוּ
אֶת מַחֲסֵנוּ
אֶת מְזִינָתֵנוּ
אֶת מַדְרִיכָתֵנוּ

קוּמוּ כָּבֶשׂ. שֶׂה, עֵז, בָּקָר
וּבוֹאוּ תַּחַת עֵץ הַחַיִּים
כִּי הֱבִיאָנוּ אֱלֹהִים אֶל אֶרֶץ טוֹבָה
אֶרֶץ שֶׁרֶב בָּהּ נְחָלִים וּבְאֵרוֹת וּמַעֲיָנוֹת
זוֹרְמִים הַמַּיִם בַּמִּישׁוֹרִים וּבַגְּבָעוֹת
אֶרֶץ שֶׁל חִטָּה וּשְׂעוֹרָה
גֶּפֶן. תְּאֵנָה וְרִמּוֹנִים
אֶרֶץ שֶׁל עֲצֵי זַיִת וּדְבַשׁ
אֶרֶץ שֶׁבָּהּ נֹאכַל לָשֹׂבַע
וְלֹא נִירָא דָבָר

לְאֵלֶּה שָׁמֵחִים בְּגָלוּת לַחֵרוּת
לְשָׁנָה הַבָּאָה בִּירוּשָׁלַיִם.

יַלְדֵי הָגָר וְשָׂרָה.
הָבָה נָשׁוּב אֶל גַּן הַחַיִּים
וְנִבְנֶה בָּתִּים חֲדָשִׁים שֶׁאֵין בָּם מִשְׁקוֹסִים

בָּרוּךְ אַתָּה יְיָ אֱלֹהֵינוּ מֶלֶךְ הָעוֹלָם הַמּוֹצִיא לֶחֶם מִן הָאָרֶץ

בְּרוּכָה עֵין הַחַיִּים הַמּוֹצִיאָה לָנוּ מָזוֹן מִן הָאָרֶץ
(וּבְשַׁבָּת אוֹמְרִים. מִי יִתֵּן וְנִזְכֶּה לְיוֹם שֶׁבּוֹ תְּהֵא שַׁבָּת לָעַד וּלְעוֹלְמֵי עוֹלָמִים.)

מַגִּישִׁים אֶת הַסְּעֻדָה

לְאַחַר הַסְּעֻדָה נִגַּשׁ צָעִיר הַיְלָדִים (אוֹ הַמְבוּגָרִים) לְחַפֵּשׂ אֶת
הָאֲפִיקוֹמָן. מִשֶּׁנִּמְצָא הָאֲפִיקוֹמָן. מִתְכַּנְּסִים כֻּלָּם לְיַד הַדֶּלֶת
הַפְּתוּחָה עִם כּוֹסוֹ שֶׁל אֵלִיָּה לְבָרֵךְ בִּרְכַּת הַמָּזוֹן.
נְבָרֵךְ אֶת הָאֵל הַחַי שֶׁאֲכַלְנוּ מִשֶּׁלוֹ וּבְטוּבוֹ חָיִינוּ. שֶׁבְּחַסְדּוֹ
וּבְרַחֲמָיו מַתְקִים כָּל חַי. וְשֶׁטּוּבוֹ יְמַלֵּא כָּל זְמַן וּמָקוֹם.

מוֹצֵא הָאֲפִיקוֹמָן זוֹכֶה לִבְצֹעַ אוֹתוֹ לְמָנוֹת וּלְחַלְּקוֹ
לַמְּסֻבִּים וּלְהַשְׁלִיךְ אֶת חֶלְקוֹ מִבַּעַד לַדֶּלֶת כְּמָזוֹן לְחַיּוֹת-
הַבַּיִת לְצִפּוֹרִים אוֹ לְחַיּוֹת הַשָּׂדֶה, וְהַכֹּל אוֹמְרִים:

שָׁמַיִם וָאָרֶץ הָיוּ לִי לְעֵדִים
כִּי הַקָּדוֹשׁ-בָּרוּךְ-הוּא
הַיּוֹשֵׁב בַּמְּרוֹמִים וּמְחַלֵּק נַחֲלוֹת
בֵּין כָּל יְלִידֵי הָעוֹלָם
מֵאֱנוֹשׁ וְעַד חַיָּה וְעַד רֶמֶשׂ.
וְעַד לְעוֹף הַשָּׁמַיִם (עַל-פִּי מִדְרָשׁ)
כָּל דִּצְרִיךְ יֵיתֵי וְיֵאָכֵל בַּלַּיְלָה הַזֶּה
כָּל דְּעַבְדִין יֵצֵא לַחָפְשִׁי בַּלַּיְלָה הַזֶּה
כָּל יְצוּר סוֹבֵל יִגָּאֵל מִיִּסּוּרָיו בַּלַּיְלָה הַזֶּה
וּלְעוֹלְמֵי עַד

חֲלוּצֵי הַמָּשִׁיחַ: הָבָה נִתְכַּנֵּס בְּפֶתַח הַדֶּלֶת, וְנַעֲמֹד עַל
כָּךְ שֶׁמְּקוֹר חַיֵּי הָרוּחַ שֶׁלָּנוּ וַחֲזוֹן הֶעָתִיד שֶׁלָּנוּ
אֶחָד הֵם. תְּנוּעָתוֹ הַחָפְשִׁית שֶׁל הַדַּחַף הַמּוּסָרִי
מְחַיֶּבֶת מַתַּן צֶדֶק לְכָל בַּעֲלֵי הַחַיִּים וּתְבִיעַת זְכֻיּוֹתֵיהֶם
חֲבוּיָה בְּרִגְשׁוֹת מֻסָרִית שֶׁבַּבְּרָבִים הָעֲמֻקִּים יוֹתֵר שֶׁל הַתּוֹרָה:
יֵהִנֵּה נָתַתִּי לָכֶם אֶת-כָּל-עֵשֶׂב זֹרֵעַ זֶרַע
אֲשֶׁר עַל-פְּנֵי כָל-הָאָרֶץ וְאֶת-כָּל-הָעֵץ אֲשֶׁר-בּוֹ פְרִי-עֵץ
זֹרֵעַ זָרַע לָכֶם יִהְיֶה לְאָכְלָה.
אֵיךְ נוּכַל אֵיפוֹא לְהַרְשׁוֹת שֶׁסְּגֻלָּה רַבַּת-עֵרֶךְ שֶׁכָּזוֹ.
אֲשֶׁר לְמַעֲשֶׂה הָיְתָה פַּעַם בִּידֵי הַמִּין הָאֱנוֹשִׁי.
תֹּאבַד לָנֶצַח? (עַל-פִּי הָרַב יִצְחָק הַכֹּהֵן קוּק)

חֲלוּצֵי הַמָּשִׁיחַ: אוֹר יִשְׂרָאֵל אֵינֶנּוּ חֲלוֹם בְּעָלְמָא, אוֹ מֻסָּרִיּוּת
מֻפְשֶׁטֶת אוֹ מִשְׁאָלָה חֲסוּדָה וְחָזוֹן נָאֱצָל. אֵין בּוֹ מִשּׁוּם
זְנִיחַת הָעוֹלָם הַחָמְרִי עַל כָּל עֲרָכָיו. נְטִישַׁת הַבָּשָׂר. וְהַחֶבְרָה
וְהַמִּמְשָׁל לְדַרְכֵיהֶם הַגְּלוּזוֹת. אֵין בּוֹ מִשּׁוּם עֲזִיבַת כּוֹחוֹת
הַטֶּבַע שֶׁנָּפְלוּ עִם נְפִילַת הַמִּין הָאֱנוֹשִׁי. נֶהְפּוֹךְ הוּא. יֵשׁ בּוֹ
מִשּׁוּם הַעֲלָאָתָם שֶׁל הַחַיִּים.

אֵין עוֹד עַם שֶׁבָּגַר דַּיּוֹ בְּרוּחוֹ וּבְנַפְשׁוֹ עַד שֶׁיּוּכַל לְהַעֲרִיךְ
אֶת קְדֻשַּׁת הַקִּיּוּם, הַשִּׂמְחָה שֶׁבְּגַדְלוּת הָאֱלֹהִים, הַמַּלְכוּת שֶׁבַּבְּרִיאָה
מִתְּחִלָּתָהּ וְעַד סוֹפָהּ, כְּפִי שֶׁהִיא נִגְלֵית בְּעוֹלָמֵנוּ דֶּרֶךְ טוֹב-לִבּוֹ
הָאֵינְסוֹפִי, עָצְמָתוֹ הָאַדִּירָה וְטָהֳרָתוֹ הַשְּׁלֵמָה שֶׁל הָאֵל הָאֶחָד.

חֲלוּצֵי הַמָּשִׁיחַ, מֹשֶׁה וְאֵלִיָּהוּ הִשְׁתַּיְּכוּ לְאוֹתָהּ פְּעֻלַּת גְּאֻלָּה,
הָאֶחָד מְיַצֵּג אֶת רֵאשִׁיתָהּ וְהַשֵּׁנִי אֶת סוֹפָהּ, כָּךְ שֶׁבְּיַחַד הֵם
מַגְשִׁימִים אֶת מַטְרָתָהּ. רוּחַ יִשְׂרָאֵל קְשׁוּבָה לְקוֹל רַחֲשׁוֹ שֶׁל
תַּהֲלִיךְ הַגְּאֻלָּה, לְגַלֵּי הַקּוֹל שֶׁל חֶבְלֵי לֵדָתוֹ שֶׁיִּסְתַּיְּמוּ
רַק בִּימֵי בּוֹא הַמָּשִׁיחַ.

הוֹדוּ לַיְיָ בּוֹרְאֵנוּ
הוֹדוּ לֵאלֹהֵי הָאֱלֹהִים
לְעוֹשֵׂה נִפְלָאוֹת גְּדֹלוֹת,
לְעוֹשֵׂה הַשָּׁמַיִם וְהָאָרֶץ
לְרוֹקַע הָאָרֶץ עַל-הַמָּיִם
לְעוֹשֵׂה אוֹרִים גְּדֹלִים בַּשָּׁמַיִם,
אֶת-הַשֶּׁמֶשׁ לְמֶמְשֶׁלֶת בַּיּוֹם וְאֶת-הַיָּרֵחַ לְמֶמְשָׁלָה בַּלָּיְלָה
לְמַכֵּה בְּפַרְעֹה הַמּוֹצִיא יִשְׂרָאֵל מֵעַבְדוּת
בְּיָד חֲזָקָה וּבִזְרוֹעַ נְטוּיָה
לְגֹזֵר יַם-סוּף לִגְזָרִים
וְהֶעֱבִיר יִשְׂרָאֵל בְּתוֹכוֹ בְּשָׁלוֹם
וְנִעֵר פַּרְעֹה וְחֵילוֹ בְיַם-סוּף
לְמוֹלִיךְ עַמּוֹ בַּמִּדְבָּר
לְמַכֵּה מְלָכִים אַדִּירִים,
סִיחוֹן מֶלֶךְ הָאֱמֹרִי
וְעוֹג מֶלֶךְ הַבָּשָׁן
וְנָתַן אַרְצָם נַחֲלָה לְיִשְׂרָאֵל
שֶׁבְּשִׁפְלֵנוּ זָכַר לָנוּ
וּמִצָּרֵינוּ שֶׁחֲרָרָנוּ

נוֹתֵן לֶחֶם לְכָל בָּשָׂר
הוֹדוּ לְאֵל הַשָּׁמַיִם
וְהָשֵׁב אוֹתָנוּ אֱלֹהִים
הֲשִׁיבֵנוּ אֵל גַּנְּךְ

יְיָ אֱלֹהַי גָּדַלְתָּ מְּאֹד
הוֹד וְהָדָר לָבָשְׁתָּ
עֹטֶה אוֹר כַּשַּׂלְמָה
נוֹטֶה שָׁמַיִם כַּיְרִיעָה
הַמְקָרֶה בַמַּיִם עֲלִיּוֹתָיו
הַשָּׂם עָבִים רְכוּבוֹ
הַמְהַלֵּךְ עַל כַּנְפֵי רוּחַ
עֹשֶׂה מַלְאָכָיו רוּחוֹת
מְשָׁרְתָיו אֵשׁ לֹהֵט
יָסַד אֶרֶץ עַל מְכוֹנֶיהָ בַּל תִּמּוֹט עוֹלָם וָעֶד
תְּהוֹם כַּלְּבוּשׁ כִּסִּיתוֹ
עַל הָרִים יַעַמְדוּ מָיִם
מִן גַּעֲרָתְךָ יְנוּסוּן
יַעֲלוּ הָרִים יֵרְדוּ בְקָעוֹת
גְּבוּל שַׂמְתָּ בַּל יַעֲבֹרוּן
בַּל יְשֻׁבוּן לְכַסּוֹת הָאָרֶץ

הַמְשַׁלֵּחַ מַעְיָנִים בַּנְּחָלִים
בֵּין הָרִים יְהַלֵּכוּן
יַשְׁקוּ כָּל חַיְתוֹ שָׂדָי
יִשְׁבְּרוּ פְרָאִים צְמָאָם
עֲלֵיהֶם עוֹף הַשָּׁמַיִם יִשְׁכּוֹן
מִבֵּין עֳפָאיִם יִתְּנוּ קוֹל
מַשְׁקֶה הָרִים מֵעֲלִיּוֹתָיו
מִפְּרִי מַעֲשֶׂיךָ תִּשְׂבַּע הָאָרֶץ
מַצְמִיחַ חָצִיר לַבְּהֵמָה
וְעֵשֶׂב לַעֲבֹדַת הָאָדָם
לְהוֹצִיא לֶחֶם מִן הָאָרֶץ
וְיַיִן יְשַׂמַּח לְבַב אֱנוֹשׁ
לְהַצְהִיל פָּנִים מִשָּׁמֶן
וְלֶחֶם לְבַב אֱנוֹשׁ יִסְעָד
יִשְׂבְּעוּ עֲצֵי יְיָ
אַרְזֵי לְבָנוֹן אֲשֶׁר נָטָע
אֲשֶׁר שָׁם צִפֳּרִים יְקַנֵּנוּ
חֲסִידָה בְּרוֹשִׁים בֵּיתָהּ
הָרִים הַגְּבֹהִים לַיְּעֵלִים
סְלָעִים מַחְסֶה לַשְׁפַנִּים

עָשָׂה יָרֵחַ לְמוֹעֲדִים
שֶׁמֶשׁ יָדַע מְבוֹאוֹ
תָּשֶׁת חֹשֶׁךְ וִיהִי לָיְלָה
בּוֹ תִרְמֹשׂ כָּל חַיְתוֹ יָעַר
הַכְּפִירִים שֹׁאֲגִים לַטָּרֶף
וּלְבַקֵּשׁ מֵאֵל אָכְלָם
תִּזְרַח הַשֶּׁמֶשׁ יֵאָסֵפוּן
וְאֶל מְעוֹנֹתָם יִרְבָּצוּן
יֵצֵא אָדָם לְפָעֳלוֹ
וְלַעֲבֹדָתוֹ עֲדֵי עָרֶב

מָה רַבּוּ מַעֲשֶׂיךָ יְיָ
כֻּלָּם בְּחָכְמָה עָשִׂיתָ
מָלְאָה הָאָרֶץ קִנְיָנֶךָ
זֶה הַיָּם גָּדוֹל וּרְחַב יָדָיִם
שָׁם רֶמֶשׂ וְאֵין מִסְפָּר חַיּוֹת
קְטַנּוֹת עִם גְּדֹלוֹת
שָׁם אֳנִיּוֹת יְהַלֵּכוּן
לִוְיָתָן זֶה יָצַרְתָּ לְשַׂחֶק בּוֹ
כֻּלָּם אֵלֶיךָ יְשַׂבֵּרוּן
לָתֵת אָכְלָם בְּעִתּוֹ

תִּפְתַּח יָדְךָ
יִשְׂבְּעוּן טוֹב
תַּסְתִּיר פָּנֶיךָ
יִבָּהֵלוּן
תֹּסֵף רוּחָם
יִגְוָעוּן וְאֶל עֲפָרָם יְשׁוּבוּן
תְּשַׁלַּח רוּחֲךָ יִבָּרֵאוּן
וּתְחַדֵּשׁ פְּנֵי אֲדָמָה

הֲשִׁיבֵנוּ. רִבּוֹן הַחַיִּים
הֲשִׁיבֵנוּ אֶל גַּנֶּךָ

אָמֵן

SHIRIM

SONG OF SONGS

Song of Songs 2:10–12

Traditional nigun

Ku - mi lah ra - ya _____ ti _____
Ha - nitz - a - nim nir - u va - a - retz

ya - fa - ti ul - hi _____ lah ki hin - nei has -
eit ha - za - mir hig - gi - a v' - kol ha - tor

tav a - var _____ ha - geh - shem ha - laf ha - lah lo.
nish - ma _____ b' - ar - tzei - nu, b' - ar - tzei - nu.

MA NISHTANA

Israeli

Ma nish - ta - na ha - lai - lah ha - zeh mi - kol ha - lei - lot, mi -

kol ha - lei - lot? She - b' - hol ha - lei - lot a - nu oh - lin 1. ha -
2. sh' -

meitz _____ u - ma - tzah, ha - meitz _____ u - ma - tzah. Ha -
ar _____ y' - ra - kot, sh' - ar _____ y - ra - kot. Ha -

lai - lah ha - zeh, ha - lai - lah ha - zeh ku - lo _____ ma - tzah, _____ ha -
lai - lah ha - zeh, ha - lai - lah ha - zeh ku - lo _____ ma - ror, _____ ha -

lai - lah ha - zeh ha - lai - lah ha - zeh ku - lo _____ ma - tzah. 2. She - b' -
lai - lah ha - zeh ha - lai - lah ha - zeh ku - lo _____ ma - ror.

3. She-b'-hol ha-lei-lot ein a-nu mat-bi-lin a-fi-lu pa-am e-hat.
Ha-lai-lah ha-zeh, ha-lai-lah ha-zeh sh'-tei f'a-a-mim.

4. She-b'-hol ha-lei-lot a-nu oh-lin bein yosh-vin u-vein m'-su-bin.
Ha-lai-lah ha-zeh, ha-lai-lah ha-zeh ku-la-nu m'-su-bin.

EILIYAHU HANAVI

Ei - li - ya - hu ha - na - vi, ei - li - ya - hu ha - tish - bi,

Fine

ei - li - ya - hu, ei - li - ya - hu, ei - li - ya - hu ha - gi - la - di.

Bim - hei - ra v' - ya - mei - nu, ya - vo ei - lei - nu

Da capo al Fine

im ma - shi - aḥ ben da - vid, im ma - shi - aḥ ben da - vid.

HAL'LU ET ADONAI KOL GOYIM

Ha - l' - lu et a - do - nai kol go - yim. Sha - b' - ḥu

hu kol ha - u - mim. Ki ga - var a - lei - nu ḥas -

do v' - e - met a - do - nai l' - o - lam. Ha - l' - lu - yah.

V'HI SHEAMDAH

Ḥasidic

V' - hi she - am - dah, v'hi she-am-dah la-a-vo-tei-nu v'-la - nu. V'-
hi she-am-dah, v'hi she-am-dah la-a-vo-tei-nu v'-la - nu. She -
lo e-ḥad bi-l'-vad a - mad a-lei-nu l'-ḥa-lo-tei-nu. She-
e-la she-b'-ḥol____ dor va-dor om-dim a-lei-nu l'-ḥa-lo-tei-nu.
V'ha-ka-dosh ba-ruḥ hu ma-tzi-lei-nu mi-ya-dam.

DAYEINU

I - lu ho-tzi ho-tzi-a - nu, ho-tzi-a-nu mi-mitz-ra-yim,
ho-tzi-a - nu mi-mitz-ra-yim da - yei - nu.
(Chorus) Da - da-yei-nu,____ da-da-yei-nu,____ da-da-yei-nu, da-
yei - nu da-yei-nu da-yei-nu. yei - nu da-yei - nu.

2. I-lu na-tan, na-tan la-nu, na-tan la-nu et ha-sha-bat, na-tan la-nu
et ha-sha-bat, dayeinu. (Chorus).

3. I-lu na-tan, na-tan la-nu, na-tan la-nu et ha-to-rah, na-tan la-nu et
ha-to-rah, dayeinu. (Chorus.)

Psalm 118:19, 17

Pit - ḥu li sha - a - rei tze - dek a - vo __ vam o - de -

yah. Lo a - mut ki eḥ - yeh ____ v'a - sa - peir ma - a - sei

yah. O - pen up, O gates __ of right - eous - ness that we may
day which God has or - dained for us. For we were

en - ter and sing Thy praise. To Thee, O God, does Is - ra - el's
des - tined of old. We lift our voice, our souls __ with -

song a - rise ____ won - drous in our eyes. This is the
in re - joice. His end - less praise be told.

AM YISRAEIL ḤAI

Folksong

Am Yis - ra - eil ḥai, am Yis - ra - eil ḥai,

am Yis - ra - eil ḥai, Ad b' - li __ dai, ad b' - li __ dai, ____

ad b' - li __ dai, ____ Am Yis - ra - eil ḥai, am Yis - ra - eil ḥai.

ḤAD GADYA

Refrain

Ḥad gad - ya, _____ ḥad gad - ya 1. di -

z' - van a - bah bit - rei ___ zu - zei. 2. V' - a - tah shun - rah
3. V' - a - tah kal - bah

v' - a - ḥal l' - gad - ya. (. . . . .) Di - z' - van a - bah
v' - na - shaḥ l' - shun - rah d' - a - ḥal l' - gad - ya.

bit - rei ___ zu - zei. 4. V' - a - tah ḥu - trah v'hi - kah l' - kal - bah d' -

no - shaḥ l' - shun - rah d' - a - ḥal l' - gad -

ya di - z' - van a - bah bit - rei ___ zu - zei.

5. V'-a-tah nu-rah v'sa-raf l'ḥu-trah.
d'hi-kah l'ḥal-bah d'na-shaḥ l'shun-rah,
d'a-ḥal l'gad-ya di-z'van a-bah bit-rei zuzei . . .

6. V'-a-tah ma-yah v'ḥa-vah l'nu-rah,
d'sa-raf l'ḥu-trah d'hi-kah l'ḥal-bah,
d'na-shaḥ l'shun-rah d'a-ḥal l'gad-ya
di-z'van a-bah bit-rei zuzei . . .

7. V'-a-tah to-rah v'sha-tah l'ma-yah,
d'ḥa-vah l'nu-rah d'sa-raf l'ḥu-trah,
d'hi-kah l'ḥal-bah d'na-shaḥ l'shun-rah,
d'a-ḥal l'gad-ya di-z'van a-bah bit-rei zuzei . . .

8. V'-a-tah ha-sho-ḥeit v'sha-ḥat l'to-rah,
d'sha-tah l'ma-yah d'ḥa-vah l'nu-rah,
d'sa-raf l'ḥu-trah, d'hi-kah l'ḥal-bah,
d'na-shaḥ l'shun-rah d'a-ḥal l'gad-ya,
di-z'van a-bah bit-rei zuzei . . .

9. V'-a-tah mal-aḥ ha-ma-vet v'sha-ḥat la-sho-ḥeit,
d'sha-ḥat l'to-rah d'sha-tah l'ma-yah,
d'ḥa-vah l'nu-rah d'sa-raf l'ḥu-trah,
d'hi-kah l'ḥal-bah d'na-shaḥ l'shun-rah,
d'a-ḥal l'gad-ya di-z'van a-bah bit-rei zuzei . . .